NEITHER EAST NOR WEST

NEITHER EAST NOR WEST

The Basic Documents
of Non-Alignment

EDITED BY
Henry M. Christman

Sheed & Ward · New York

Copyright © 1973 by Henry M. Christman

Library of Congress Cataloging in Publication Data

Conference of Heads of State or Government of Non-aligned
 Countries.
 Neither East nor West.

 Selected addresses and documents from the 1st-3d
Conferences, held in 1961, 1964, and 1970.
 1. World politics—1945–   —Congresses.
I. Christman, Henry M., ed. II. Title.
D839.2.C65 1970   327   72-6689
ISBN 0-8362-0500-6
ISBN 0-8362-0511-1 (pbk.)

CONTENTS

v

INTRODUCTION

Leaders of sixty-two nations—one-half of the countries of the world, one-third of all mankind—convened in Lusaka, Zambia, during September, 1970, for the third conference of non-aligned countries.

This historic meeting climaxed a decade of growing cooperation and coordination among the so-called third world nations that reject the concept and the politics of a globe divided and dominated by East and West power blocs.

The non-alignment perspective officially appeared on the international scene with "The Initiative of the Five," an appeal to decrease tension between the United States and the Soviet Union, submitted as a joint draft resolution to the United Nations by President Josip Broz Tito of Yugoslavia, Prime Minister Jawaharlal Nehru of India, President Ahmed Sukarno of Indonesia, President Kwame Nkrumah of Ghana, and President Gamal Abdel Nasser of the United Arab Republic on September 30, 1960.

In only one year, this group of five nations had grown to twenty-eight states, the leaders of which gathered at the founding First Conference of Heads of State or Government of Non-Aligned Countries, held in Belgrade from September 1 through September 6, 1961.

Within three years, the non-alignment movement had expanded to fifty-seven nations, the leaders of which participated in the second conference, in Cairo, from October 5 through October 10, 1964.

By the time that the third conference met in Lusaka from September 8 through September 10, 1970, significant changes had taken place within the non-alignment movement. Of the five charismatic leaders who signed "The Initiative of the Five" in 1960, only President Tito of Yugoslavia remained on the international scene. The change in international personalities was paralleled by political changes within the non-alignment movement. Most of the national liberation movements throughout the world had accomplished their initial goal of political independence. These new nations were now grappling with post-independence national problems in the economic and social areas.

The representation of sixty-two nations at Lusaka demonstrated graphically and dramatically that the non-alignment movement not only had survived this crucial transitional period but indeed had grown further.

So much for the basic facts and statistics of the non-alignment movement. What of its policies, its goals, its significance?

The non-alignment concept is not a simplistic "anti" movement, a movement merely opposed to the division of the world into power blocs. It has clear-cut policies and goals concerning peace, disarmament, national sovereignty, colonialism, neo-colonialism, racism, and economic development.

The very diversity of the nations participating in the non-alignment movement, ranging from militantly revolutionary regimes to extremely traditionalist monarchies, emphasizes the significance of their unanimity in defining what they insist are the real issues and priorities facing the entire world.

It must be stressed that the leaders of the non-aligned nations, in their joint declarations and individual statements, are not simply representing their own countries or even the "third world" as a whole; they are endeavoring to promote new perspectives and programs for the benefit of all nations and all mankind.

In the pages that follow, the non-alignment movement speaks for itself authoritatively, eloquently, and officially.

There is no need to recapitulate here. However, a paragraph from the Lusaka Declaration on Peace, Independence, Development, Cooperation and Democratization of International Relations provides a striking introduction to the aspirations of the non-alignment movement:

Our era is at the crossroads of history; with each passing day we are presented with fresh evidence of the exceptional power of the human mind and also of the dangerous paths down which its imperfections may lead. The epoch-making scientific and technological revolution has opened up unlimited vistas of progress; at the same time, prosperity has failed to become accessible to all and a major section of mankind still lives under conditions unworthy of man. Scientific discoveries and their application to technology have the possibility of welding the world into an integral whole, reducing the distance between countries and continents to a measure making international cooperation increasingly indispensable and ever more possible; yet the states and nations comprising the present international community are still separated by political, economic and racial barriers. These barriers divide countries into developed and the developing, oppressors and the oppressed, the aggressors and the victims of aggression; into those who act from positions of strength, either military or economic, and those who are forced to live in the shadow of permanent danger of covert and overt assaults on their independence and security. In spite of the great progressive achievements and aspirations of our generation, neither peace, nor prosperity, nor the right to independence and equality, have yet become the integral, indivisible attribute of all mankind. Our age, however, raises the greatest hopes and also presents the greatest challenges.

Henry M. Christman

New York and Belgrade

The Belgrade Conference

SEPTEMBER 1–6, 1961

OPENING ADDRESS BY
PRESIDENT JOSIP BROZ TITO
OF YUGOSLAVIA

I am gratified to be able to extend to you, on behalf of the government and peoples of Yugoslavia, our warmest greetings and wish you a pleasant stay in our country. Our peoples consider it a great honor to have such a distinguished gathering take place in Yugoslavia, particularly the citizens of Belgrade, which has, throughout its long history, seen many wars of conquest, invasions and invaders, and which has now, for the first time, the opportunity to welcome, in its midst, the highest representatives of twenty-seven countries—champions of peace.

I particularly wish to express to all of you our sincere gratitude for your personal efforts and your contribution which have made it possible to have this gathering organized and convened in such a brief period of time. Considering the tremendous responsibilities that every one of you, as a statesman, has in his own country, your presence here demonstrates most explicitly your concern and the concern of your peoples for the fate of mankind and your wish to exert concerted efforts in the existing grave international situation in order to find a way out of the crisis in which the world finds itself at present.

In a few days it will be exactly one year that a large number of heads of state and government of many countries assembled at the fifteenth session of the General Assembly of the United Nations for the purpose of helping to ease, by their participation, the grave international situation and contribute to the maintenance of peace. At the said session the non-aligned countries displayed for the first time their firm determination to exert resolute efforts towards the peaceful and correct solution of international disputes as well as their resolution not to allow anyone to play with the fate of mankind in an irresponsible manner. No one can deny the fact that this first concerted action of non-aligned countries was successful. In the first place, a tremendous moral success was achieved. However, today, one year later, we must, unfortunately, note that the situation is much worse, as the cold war has assumed proportions liable to lead to the greatest tragedy at any moment. Precisely because of this, it is necessary for the representatives of non-aligned countries to examine on the highest level, in a more detailed manner and in greater numbers, the dangerous international situation and to take, in this connection, coordinated action, primarily through the United Nations, in order to find a way out of the present situation and to prevent the outbreak of a new military conflict. The fact that this danger has reached its climax is clearly shown by all the preparations which are now being undertaken. Overt preparations for war are being made, mobilization is taking place, the manufacture of the most up-to-date weapons is being intensified, hydrogen and atomic weapons tests are again being contemplated, etc. Only recently we have witnessed an open military aggression against an independent state—Tunisia, where the unrestrained French *soldatesque* has not only shed much of the blood of the innocent civilian population of Bizerta, but is, at the same time, continuously threatening both the integrity and independence of Tunisia.

Never in the entire post-war period has it been so urgently necessary as today that states which are not aligned with any bloc should set forth with the greatest degree of unanimity, clearly and unequivocally, through their highest representatives, their views on problems which are leading the whole world to the brink of the greatest catastrophe in its history. The idea that non-aligned countries should participate, in one way or another, more effectively in international developments, particularly in those which are of direct and vital interest to them, stems from the realization of the fact that, in our time, the responsibility for the future of mankind cannot be borne only by a few states, irrespective of how large and powerful they may be.

The Bandung conference and the principles proclaimed there were, after the adoption of the Charter of the United Nations, the first powerful display of this contemporary view of international relations. It was no accident that these principles were proclaimed precisely in Asia, in the presence of the representatives of the peoples of Asia and Africa, the two continents inhabited by the largest number of people on our planet, who had been enslaved, deprived of rights and subject to discrimination through many centuries. The Casablanca conference also reflected the determination of the peoples of Africa to decide themselves about their own fate and not to tolerate any longer the existence of any form of colonialism on African soil. In the same way as the Bandung conference, and other similar conferences which followed, did not intend to establish any kind of bloc, the present conference does not pursue any such aim either. On the contrary, this conference should adopt a negative attitude towards bloc exclusiveness, which not only constitutes a threat to world peace, but also prevents other countries from participating as equal partners in the solving of outstanding international issues. The fact that discrimination of this kind against these countries is gradually diminishing is, to a large extent, the result of a greater measure of unity of action on the part of the non-aligned countries with regard to various problems which are endangering world peace.

As a result of the experience acquired in the post-war period, when groupings of individual states began to emerge, all the countries outside these groupings have become profoundly convinced that increasing tensions in the world have been, and are still, arising precisely from this division of the world. This conviction is also shared by the broadest masses of people, regardless of whether they are inside or outside the blocs, as they feel that the mechanism of the blocs is acquiring, to an increasing extent, its own pernicious logic. This division has demonstrated that outstanding international problems cannot be solved from a position of strength. Actually, constant efforts are being exerted for the purpose of achieving superiority, in order to attain specific goals from a position of strength, that is to say, to solve outstanding questions in one's own favor. In this precisely lies the greatest danger of an outbreak of armed conflict and of a new catastrophe of the entire world. The recent past has shown clearly that the grouping of states into blocs usually leads to a settling of accounts by the force of arms. The history of recent years has also demonstrated that there need not even be two blocs, but that it is sufficient to have only one bloc for war to break out.

I think that it is well-known how, in what order and for what purpose the existing military blocs were established and I do not intend to analyze this matter in greater detail here at the present moment. However, it is obvious that such a course was most unfortunate and has led to the present abnormal and perilous situation in the world. I feel, therefore, that it is high time to have this division removed, at least gradually, and to embark upon a new and fresh road of understanding and cooperation in international relations by means of peaceful negotiations. However, the best way of proceeding would be to settle outstanding issues through the United Nations; and it is precisely for that purpose that the world organization was created.

Such a practice in international relations in keeping with our times has already been put into effect by countries non-aligned with any blocs. At this conference also, attended by such a great number of heads of state or government of non-aligned countries, new standards governing relations among states should fully prevail. On the agenda are problems of exceptional and major importance, problems that the great powers have failed to solve so far, precisely because they approached them in the old way. In this connection an obsolete and, in the present phase, extremely dangerous conception of prestige is still playing a crucial role. Furthermore, there still prevails, as in the past, the practice that only the biggest, the most advanced and militarily the most powerful countries attempt to make decisions involving the fate of the world, while a large number of small and medium-sized countries, which are not developed for well-known reasons but constitute the majority of mankind, have been unable, until recently, to participate as equal partners in the taking of decisions on questions of general interest. These countries were looked upon, and are even today considered, as a kind of reserve and voting machine in international forums, such as the United Nations and others. This gathering of the highest representatives of non-aligned countries illustrates, however, that such outdated practices must be discarded, that non-aligned countries can no longer reconcile themselves with the status of observers and voters and that, in their opinion, they have the right to participate in the solving of problems, particularly of those which endanger the peace and the fate of the world at the present moment. This meeting has been convened, *inter alia,* for the purpose of asserting this right. The non-aligned countries do not, of course, pretend to be able to solve alone the problems that the great powers have not been able to solve so far; however, they can contribute much both towards this end and towards the easing of dangerous international tensions in general. The adoption at this meeting of clear and unequivocal positions on current problems of vital importance will make it easier for the great powers to approach more realistically the task of reaching agreement on outstanding issues and to pay greater attention to the views of the representatives of countries which are not aligned with blocs and whose strivings are shared by the majority of mankind.

Fears that this meeting might mark the beginning of the formation of a third bloc are groundless. Would it be logical for us, who are fighting against the division of the world into blocs, to create a third bloc? Would this contribute towards the relaxation of tension in the world? Of course not. We cannot pursue such aims as they would run counter to the political concept of non-aligned countries. If we examine the actual substance of blocs, their characteristic features, we find that their first and most important feature is their military aspect, the creation of military power. An unrelenting arms race is being pursued in order to gain superiority. The economic arrangements within bloc frameworks have a discriminatory character in regard to other countries. Embargoes are imposed on various products with the aim of exercising pressure upon a given country or several countries. All this and many other characteristic features of blocs are in contradiction with the general interests and views of non-aligned countries and, above all, with the fact that these countries preclude the use of military force for the solution of any dispute. This will suffice to demonstrate that it is absurd to impute to this Conference of Heads of State or Government of Non-Aligned Countries the intention to set up a third bloc.

The purpose of this meeting is to make the great powers realize that the fate of the world cannot rest in their hands alone. It is to demonstrate to the protagonists of force that the majority of the world decisively rejects the use of force as a means for settling the various important problems we have inherited from the last war. I can state without exaggeration that the countries represented at this conference, as well as many others which do not belong to any grouping, represent the great majority of world public opinion. They represent the conscience of mankind. Those who are contemplating war adventures must bear this in mind. Such an example was also provided by the Second World War. This war ended disastrously for the mightiest fascist states, which had made tyranny and force the guiding principle of their policy, and war a means for achieving their aims, that is, for imposing their domination upon the entire world—ignoring humane and other moral principles which are asserting themselves with increasing force in the present-day world. The political conceptions and aggressive ventures of the Axis powers aroused the entire peace-loving world, and this was bound to lead to the defeat of the powerful and, at that time, the mightiest military machine. The moral of this story is very instructive and it should be borne in mind by those who are indulging in saber-rattling and are holding the world in a state of constant tension and fear.

May I now draw your attention to a fallacy which makes its appearance from time to time, in the press and in commentaries in general, regarding the course that the Conference of Heads of State or Government of Non-Aligned Countries will take: Whether or not this course will be pro-Western or pro-Eastern. There is no ground for such speculations because we have not met here in order to support blocs, but to define clearly and coordinate our positions on the most important problems which are besetting the world today. And then it will become clear where our stands differ and where they coincide with those of one or the other side. On all the most important issues we shall adopt positions which will be not only in the interest of non-aligned countries but will be, generally speaking, in the interest of peace and of the entirety of mankind. They will, in our submission, contribute to the lessening of dangers to peace and will show to world public opinion that there is a better way towards understanding than the threats of war.

Similarly there is no ground for assuming that this or that country will be attacked here. It would be erroneous if we were to attack certain countries here, as such, for purely propaganda motives, instead of voicing our resolute disagreement with the methods applied by some great powers towards other countries. Because, if we were to act in this way, we would not bring about a relaxation of tension in the world, but would, on the contrary, add to the tension. There is no doubt that we shall examine such problems as the question of colonialism in a consistent and serious manner; we shall pose this question in a clear form and insist on the final and early eradication of colonialism. The question of disarmament and use of atomic resources for military purposes, the problem of assistance to less developed countries and others should be examined here in the same manner.

I believe that we all agree that the success of the conference depends precisely on our consensus of views regarding these major questions of paramount importance for the safeguarding of peace. There are also other issues of secondary importance. On some of them it is not easy to reach agreement and they could, if insisted upon, impair the success of the conference. I am referring in particular to disputes between some of the non-aligned countries. In my view we should for the solution of such questions have recourse to the method of bilateral negotiations, on the basis of peaceful understanding, a method which should be proper to non-aligned countries and which is in harmony with our principles.

This meeting does not necessarily require us to reach unanimity on all questions. But it would be extremely useful to reach unanimity on those problems which are at this moment of vital importance for all mankind—and I am convinced that the world is expecting this from us.

Therefore, in the present extremely tense international situation this conference is the most competent forum, outside the United Nations, where the representatives of non-aligned countries can state, as simply and as strongly as possible, their views regarding the question as to what the relations among peoples and states should be like and as to how the solution of outstanding issues by peaceful means could and should be brought about without thereby impairing but rather promoting world peace and constructive cooperation among peoples.

Assembled here at this conference, we are conscious that we are taking upon ourselves a great responsibility before the peace-loving world, which rightly hopes that we shall do everything in our power here in order to remove the danger which is hovering over mankind. The peoples of all the world are expecting to hear a unanimous and resolute call against all that hampers the peaceful creative life of people on earth. People are already tired of the cold war, which is assuming ever sharper forms, and they fear the possible catastrophe which could be caused by a new world war. Therefore, I feel that we shall render a great service to the world if we indicate clearly and resolutely the road towards a relaxation of world tensions and to the freedom, equality and peaceful cooperation of all nations.

ADDRESS BY
PRESIDENT AHMED SUKARNO
OF INDONESIA

Allow me, first of all, to extend my heartfelt thanks to you, President Tito, and through you to the government and people of the Federal Republic of Yugoslavia for the warm reception extended to us all at this conference. As you well know, I myself feel perfectly at home in this great country, and I am sure that my fellow participants will enjoy their stay here because of the friendliness and hospitality of the people.

May I also at this point extend heartfelt thanks to all those who have worked on the preparations for this conference. The preparatory conference in Cairo did very important spadework. The work they did in formulating an agreed set of criteria for non-alignment and in drafting an agenda for our meeting, as well as their suggestions regarding the organizational aspects of the conference, have greatly helped to ensure us success.

It was only a few short months ago that I, together with my good friends, President Tito of Yugoslavia and President Nasser of the United Arab Republic, took the initiative in calling for the convening of a conference of non-aligned countries. Our initiative was based on the conviction that non-alignment has become a growing force in the world, a force standing for friendship among nations, for peace, for social justice, and that the time has now come to gather this force together, to turn it into a coordinated, accumulated moral force.

We made this call in the conviction that such a conference was needed, that it would evoke widespread response, but speaking for myself—and I am sure that my co-initiators will agree—the actual response to our call has surpassed our expectations.

We come together here not as members of a bloc, for indeed countries which conduct a policy of non-alignment do not constitute a bloc. We abhor the very idea of blocs. We have come together because we maintain the view that the creation of blocs, especially when based upon power politics and the armaments race, can only lead to war which, in this nuclear era, can only mean the extinction of mankind.

There was no prior consultation and agreement between us before we adopted our respective policies of non-alignment. No. We each arrived at this policy inspired by common ideals, prompted by similar circumstances, spurred on by like experiences. There was no attempt at compromise among us, no attempt to round off disagreements to make our policies identical. But not one of us, I think, will deny that we did inspire each other. The experiences of one country in discovering that a policy of non-alignment is the best guarantee for safeguarding our national and international position have undoubtedly helped others to come to a similar conclusion.

Non-alignment is not directed against any one country or against any one bloc or against any particular type of social system. It is our common conviction that a policy of non-alignment is the best way for each of us to make a positive contribution towards the preservation of peace and the relaxation of international tensions.

And let us be quite frank. It is not mere accident that we countries gathered here happen to be the ones who have set ourselves on the path of non-alignment. Every nation, without exception, basically desires such a policy, knows that it could help preserve world peace by the adoption of such a policy. But the possibility to conduct a policy of non-alignment depends not upon desire alone. It may be that because of historical background, because of the immediate national interest, because of the geographical position, many countries do not have the opportunity, or even the capacity, to conduct a policy of non-alignment.

The idea of convening this conference, as I have said, was born but a few months ago, but the idea of non-alignment is not new. It is an idea that has inspired many nations for many years. I am indeed proud that the Republic of Indonesia was one of its first protagonists. Ever since our Proclamation of Independence in 1945, our foreign policy has been based upon, inspired by, the principles of non-alignment. The following words are from the preamble of our constitution drawn up in 1945:

. . . to set up a government of the State of Indonesia which shall . . . contribute in implementing an order in the world which is based upon independence, abiding peace and social justice.

My presence here in this conference, which has the full and united backing of the entire Indonesian people, is in fulfillment of these profound words.

We who are participating in this conference come from all parts of the globe. We come from Europe, from Asia, from Africa, from Latin America. Our peoples are different in many ways, our cultures differ, our forms of state differ, and so do our political systems. But in an essential way we do not differ, and that is in our determination to implement a new order in the world which is based upon independence, abiding peace and social justice. We do not differ in our determination to have the freedom to be free.

Yes, ladies and gentlemen, independence, abiding peace, social justice, the freedom to be free. These are noble aims indeed. Independence means putting an end forever to the exploitation of nation by nation, indirect exploitation as well as direct exploitation. Abiding peace means, not the mere absence of war; it means removing the sources of conflict which threaten the world and split it into camps. Social justice means justice for all nations, not for one nation alone, not for one power alone, not for one group of nations or one power bloc alone. The freedom to be free means the freedom to determine our own national policies, to formulate our own national concepts, unhampered and unhindered by pressure or intervention from outside. It is the freedom to conduct our political, economic and social affairs in line with our own national concepts. It is the freedom to co-operate with all nations, to be friends with all nations, the freedom to oppose anything which harms the rightful and just interests of any nation.

These are the principles towards which we are aiming. Inevitably, they will bring us into conflict with the vested interests of the past. Yes, with the vested interests of the past. Our own bitter experience teaches us that the old equilibrium is based upon the domination of a few nations over the vast majority of mankind. And within nations, too, the ruling few live their lives of affluence and luxury at the expense of the millions who live in poverty and misery. This old equilibrium is seething with social revolt, the revolt of subjected nations against the domination of other powers, the revolt of the subjected majority against the ruling few.

From this point of view non-alignment is not neutrality. Let there be no confusion on that score. No, non-alignment is not neutrality. It is not the sanctimonious attitude of the man who holds himself aloof—"a plague on both your houses." Non-aligned policy is not a policy of seeking for a neutral position in case of war; non-aligned policy is not a policy of neutrality without its own color; being non-aligned does not mean becoming a buffer state between the two giant blocs. Non-alignment is active devotion to the lofty cause of independence, abiding peace, social justice, and the freedom to be free. It is the determination to serve this cause; it runs congruent with the social conscience of man.

And now, if non-alignment is to become the coordinated

accumulated moral force we need, powerful enough to make its impact felt upon the two conflicting blocs, powerful enough to call a halt, to save the world from catastrophe, it must be based upon a common approach to the basic issues confronting our world today—a new approach that will startle mankind by its freshness, its frank recognition of objective reality, its resolution to grapple with world problems, its determination to cut the Gordian knots strangulating international relations at the present time.

Yes, to call a halt, before it is too late! For time is running short. Many problems demand immediate solution, and as long as we fail to get to the source of the tension and strife we shall be working like amateur plumbers, plugging up a leak here only to find a bigger one spurting up behind our very backs, and another, and yet another.

We must get to the source of the tension and strife, and to do this, we must first have a common understanding of what the source is. Prevailing world opinion today would have us believe that the real source of international tension and strife is ideological conflict between the great powers. I think that is not true. There is a conflict which cuts deeper into the flesh of man, and that is the conflict between the new emergent forces for freedom and justice and the old forces of domination, the one pushing its head relentlessly through the crust of the earth which has given it its life-blood, the other striving desperately to retain all it can, trying to hold back the course of history.

As I said in my address before the United Nations General Assembly last year, this is the era of emerging nations and the turbulence of nationalism, the building of nations and the breaking of empires.

Of course, I do not deny that there is an ideological conflict between the great powers. To deny that would indeed be an ostrich-like approach. But this ideological conflict need not lead to tension. It must not lead to tension. It can take place peacefully, provided that it does not extend to an attempt to force one's own ideologies upon other nations. The problem of ideology is for every separate nation to decide, and if there is conflict, it is a conflict within the nation. Certainly ideological conflict within nations can bring turbulence, growth, more turbulence, and finally—so long as that nation is left alone to resolve its own conflicts—it will surely lead to a synthesis, a single nation-wide approach inspired by the common desire burning in the hearts of men and women everywhere to win prosperity, to establish social justice and to live in peace. Ideological conflict between nations can and must proceed peacefully, it can and must be waged not on the battlefield but on the construction site, not with nuclear weapons and napalm bombs but with bulldozers and antibiotics.

We in Indonesia know from experience that we could only arrive at our national progressive ideology, we could only consolidate this ideology, through struggle, through turbulence. And is this not also the experience of the United Arab Republic, of Iraq and of many other countries today, or, to go further back in history, of the Soviet Union, of the United States of America, of Great Britain? Every nation that sincerely strives to build a nationhood based on the concepts of prosperity and social justice will always have to go through struggle and turbulence. And inevitably, victory will be in the hands of the majority fighting for equality, against oppression, for freedom from the yoke of poverty, misery and exploitation.

Permit me, for a moment, to speak at greater length about our experiences in Indonesia. Yes, we in Indonesia have already passed through the grueling process of forming our national ideology and we have now reached our synthesis, i.e. Indonesian socialism. This inner search brought with it conflicts and commotion, an inevitable part of the process. Some people scoffed at us, complaining that we are forever arguing, caught up in endless bickering. To these people I always say: "Look back for a moment at your own histories. Did you not have years of turbulence and turmoil, your years of finding yourselves and setting yourselves on the right path?"

Yes, our Indonesian socialism developed through turmoil. In the course of that turmoil we have learned many things, and we believe that the lessons we have learned will be of interest to other nations. We have learned that the basic ingredient of any national ideology must be the national inheritance of that nation itself, its heritage from the past, the traditions which bind its people together and set the pattern of their life. In Indonesia, this is *kerakjatan, gotong royong, musjawarah* and *mufakat*—the people as the source, collective effort for a common goal, discussion and deliberation, consensus of opinion. To this basic ingredient add all useful ideas from other countries. In Indonesia, for example, we drew the equality of men from the Jefferson declaration, the American Declaration of Independence written by Thomas Jefferson; we drew spiritual socialism from Islam and Christianity; we drew scientific socialism from Marxism. Put this mixture into the mold of the national identity and the result is a national ideology which binds the people together and frees all energies for the tremendous tasks of construction.

In this process we also learned another lesson, a lesson I believe to be of immense importance. We learned that when external forces sought to bear pressure on us in our ideological conflict, turmoil and turbulence turned into hostility, violence and war. But when left to our own devices, turmoil and turbulence led to synthesis and new advance. Many of the new, emergent countries are now engaged in a similar process. Left alone, they will reach their synthesis.

So, ladies and gentlemen, recognize the world situation of today as a temporary situation; recognize it as a state of relentless movement and progress. Do not be obsessed by the conflict of ideologies. This is a matter which must be left to each nation itself. Recognize that the conflict between the new, emergent forces and the old forces of domination is today coming more and more into prominence. And this is not fortuitous. It is coming more into prominence precisely because the new, emergent forces are thrusting themselves more and more persistently upon the world, while the old forces still strive to preserve the old equilibrium, based upon the exploitation of nation by nation, based upon *l'exploitation de l'homme par l'homme.*

It is not fortuitous either that the non-aligned countries ally themselves with these new, emergent forces. It is not fortuitous that the flags that color our meeting-hall today are all flags of nations which stand in the very forefront of these new, emergent forces. They are nations which are or have been engaged in the struggle for national independence. They are nations which are determined to leave behind the inglorious past of colonization. They are nations fighting for a glorious future, a future of independence, a future of prosperity for all nations, a future of the rule of justice among nations. If we consider for a moment the positive and constructive uses to which science and technology can be put today, this is the only future which can save mankind from the danger of the silent, seething anger of the oppressed peoples exploding into the face of the world.

The world must recognize this conflict between the old and the new, recognize the existence of this conflict, and recognize all it means. Socialist states have emerged. Newly independent states have emerged—and with what tremendous speed in the past few years, with what tremendous speed! And side by side with this, science and technology have taken gigantic strides, achieving breathless new successes, while at the same time winning smaller but no less significant victories every day in the battle of mankind to master the forces of nature and harness them to meet the rising demands, the rising expectations of people everywhere.

These factors are living realities in the world today; their contours line the political and economic map of the world. But these contours are changing very fast, they need continual re-mapping if we are to keep up with reality.

The world must recognize that the new, emergent countries as a coordinated accumulated force are striving for the speedy establishment of a new stable equilibrium.

What do we mean by this new stable equilibrium? We mean that all nations must become independent. All nations must have the freedom to be free, the freedom to arrange their own national life in accordance with their own wishes, the freedom to be free to build their own national foundation—politically, economically, culturally. We mean that all nations must be free to arrange their international relations as they see fit, based on the principles of equality, justice and mutual benefit. We mean that no power shall interfere in the struggle of any other nation to find its own national concept, that no power shall attempt to force any other nation to change its ideology.

Reflect for a moment. Let us suppose that foreign intervention had played a forceful and dominant role in the American Civil War. Had that been the case, could America have become one of the leading world powers that it is today? Could America have succeeded in establishing a nation-state on the basis of which to build a national life for the American people?

In this new stable equilibrium there can and will be no place for conflicting blocs. The very notion of military alliances will become obsolete. Then truly shall we be able to speak of abiding peace.

The establishment of this new stable equilibrium can only come about with the active and conscious desire of all humanity. But can we stand idly by, waiting for this conscious desire to evolve on its own, to appear before us like a wondrous miracle, like manna from heaven? It is for the non-aligned countries, as a moral force which can take the lead, to make the establishment of this equilibrium its sacred cause, the cause to which all the energies of our accumulated strength must now be devoted.

This then, Mr. Chairman, is our objective, the target we set before ourselves. But before we can proceed, we must set our sights accurately. Where do we stand now? What are the demands of the present situation?

There is a great variety of social systems in the world— absolute monarchies, parliamentary monarchies, parliamentary democracies, socialist and communist democracies, dictatorships. Look at the great variety of social systems in Europe alone. What sharp differences there are between the one and the other. And yet, they co-exist. Yes, they co-exist, and they have co-existed for the past decades.

But at the same time, sources of tension disturb the international scene every day. Not a day passes but the columns of our newspapers blare forth news of war dangers here, there —South Africa! Congo! Cuba! Algeria! Angola! Tunisia! Berlin! The people desire to co-exist, and they *can* co-exist. But what, then, is it that causes these "trouble spots," that sends sensation-thirsty news correspondents rushing at top speed halfway around the world, hoping to be "in at the kill"?

In every single case, the cause, the root of international tension, is imperialism and colonialism and the forcible division of nations. Yes, imperialism and colonialism and the forcible division of nations! History in the past and the realities of today prove that different social systems can co-exist, but there can be no co-existence between independence and justice on one side and imperialism-colonialism on the other side.

The emergence of nations, their tenacious fight to preserve the independence they have won at so much sacrifice, their resolve to end economic servility, is a process which meets with the resistance of the old forces of domination at every turn. But this resistance is blind, it is a resistance that refuses to recognize reality, refuses to recognize the march of history. The old forces of domination must be made to realize this. Let us be quite frank. These old forces play on the fears of their own people, play on their ignorance of the stark realities of colonialism, play on their suspicions. They say, "These Africans, these Asians, these Latin Americans, they are a bunch of communists."

We non-aligned countries of the world, recognizing and accepting the reality of the emergent nations, have the bounden duty to win the understanding of the peoples in other countries, to tell them quite frankly that they cannot go on living at the expense of millions of poverty-stricken peoples. Their affluent societies are built upon the sweat and toil and tears of millions who spend their evenings not with their eyes glued upon television sets but in a darkness pierced by the flame of a single candle, whose days are tormented not by the desire to have a better car than their neighbor but the desire to give their children one meager bowl of rice a day.

We must tell them that the emergence of new nations does not threaten their affluence. Far from it. But it will require adaptations. Their rising living standards must be the result of their own hard work. The emergent nations, freed from the shackles of exploitation, freed to build their own economies, will be extremely profitable trading partners. If allowed to dispose of their own products under reasonable and stable conditions, they will raise endless demands, keeping the factories of the advanced countries buzzing night and day without fear of crisis or unemployment. Ours is a revolution of rising demands. Emergent nations demand not only independence and non-interference. They demand goods, equipment, the wherewithal to build their own industries. Do not fear us as competitors. Welcome us as emancipated partners. Together we can build an affluent world with a boundless future before it.

These are the realities of today, the realities of the future. Do not, then, try to scare us from our chosen path.

"Beware of new colonialism," the old colonial powers used to say. "If we, the old colonialism, move out, new colonialism from other countries is waiting behind the door to suffocate you in its embrace." What a lie! Let us not permit others to use the pretext of seemingly impending imperialism as a defense for existing colonialism and imperialism. This is not so!

Have no fear, gentlemen. We are not children. We know a colonialist when we see one. We shall deal as effectively with new colonialism as we have dealt with and are dealing with the old ones. Do not try to divert our attention from the present cancers rankling our bodies. Rid the world of these festering sores—Algeria, West Irian, Angola, Bizerta—and have no fear. We shall be well steeled in the battle against colonialism in its purest form. We shall be well equipped to deal with any new imperialism that may try to rear its ugly head.

On the other hand, beware of colonialism in a new cloak, the so-called neo-colonialism. This is also an item to be dealt with on our agenda, because this is a real danger.

It is common knowledge to us all that the old colonial powers, in having to leave their colonial territories, want to preserve as much as possible of their economic—and sometimes also their political and military—interests. This is carried out in various ways: By creating strife among all layers of the local people; by provoking the secession of one part of the old colonial territory from the rest under the pretext of self-determination; creating chaos through military provocation or—and this is also common—by fortifying their economic interests at the last moment, using even the most unscrupulous of means.

This is a process which we have seen, and still are seeing, in the newly independent countries. Yes, in Indonesia we have experienced it. Our people have suffered from it, and only after uniting all our national energy did we succeed in pushing back the forces of neo-colonialism and finally manage to lay down our solid national foundations. According to our experience the effective answer is national unity; I say again, national unity. This could be achieved through a national, progressive ideology which does not leave much room for the playing off of one section of the community against the other. This can be dealt with effectively by trying to understand and trying to implement the revolutionary demand of the people as a whole for a better living standard— or at least by providing them with a solid hope for the future that after independence their misery is a problem which can be solved. This can be dealt with through firm and wise national leadership.

And what about the forcible division of nations to which I referred just now? These nations forcibly divided stand on the very frontiers of the two blocs. They are nations which have been particularly severely subjected to the pull of opposing ideologies. They have been pulled so hard in opposing directions that their states have split in two. Now we have two Germanies, not one; now we have two Koreas, not one; now we have two Vietnams, not one. Even here we have seen that co-existence is possible, that these artificially divided states can live side by side in peace, and can even peaceably trade with each other. This is a good beginning. It augurs well for reunification. But the basic requirement for reunification is that the big powers must cease to treat these divided countries as ideological battlegrounds. Leave the nations to settle this matter themselves. As elsewhere, this will be a tumultuous process, a grueling process, but it will bring the desired synthesis—provided the nations concerned are left alone, again, provided they are left alone.

I have deliberately spoken at some length about the evils and injustice of the past, the achievements of the present as the result of relentless struggle and the common goals of the future. I have done this so that we should not forget. Let us never forget the misery of colonial bondage though we are now already independent. Let us never forget the misery and degradation of being poor though we our selves are living better lives. Let us never forget the misery and emptiness of illiteracy though we ourselves now possess skills and erudition. Let us never forget our past miseries, sufferings and frustrations. Were we to do so our national independence would become an obstacle in the way of the struggle of progressive forces for peace, justice and the brotherhood of mankind.

A glance at the agenda of this conference clearly shows that the basic problems besetting the present-day world arise from two radical processes in the history of mankind. Firstly, the process of liberation of the colonized people and, secondly, the process of emancipation of all nations from poverty and injustice. These two processes go hand in hand; they are inseparable. They are like Siamese twins; try to separate them from each other and both will die.

I have already spoken at length about the process of liberation. Not a single person in this hall would dispute the fact that colonialism must be eradicated, completely, irrevocably, for our own sakes and for the sake of the whole world. There is no power on earth that can stem this tide of liberation.

We must demand the immediate cessation of the colonial wars now raging in Angola, Algeria and Tunisia. We must not rest a moment until we have stopped these wars, until we have halted this criminal bloodshed and terror, all perpetrated in order to preserve the old order. We must demand that a time limit be imposed for the complete removal of all forms of colonial subjugation of one nation by another. In the case of every single remaining colonial regime that time limit must not exceed two years and must if possible be less than that.

As you know, we in Indonesia still have a colonial problem because one-fifth of the territory of our republic is still occupied and dominated by the Dutch colonialists. It is the territory of West Irian, as you know. West Irian is an indivisible part of the sovereign territory of the Republic of Indonesia and we demand that the authority of the republic be established in that region forthwith. During the past few years we have been strengthening ourselves in order to face the Dutch in all fields and we feel now quite strong enough to take all measures necessary in order to be able to unfurl our beloved red and white flag on the soil of West Irian. As I have said repeatedly, we are prepared to negotiate with the Dutch on the question of West Irian, but only if such negotiations are based on the principle of the transfer of the administration of West Irian to the Republic of Indonesia. We insist that this thorn cutting deep into our flesh must be removed at the earliest possible moment because it is a serious danger not only to our independence and stability but also to peace in Asia and the world. We demand that this problem be solved within the shortest possible time.

It was in order to contribute to world peace and to solve the West Irian problem peacefully that I offered the hand of friendship to the Dutch a few weeks ago. I offered that we should not talk any more about whose sovereignty West Irian is under but that the Dutch should transfer the government administration over West Irian to us in the shortest possible time. The Indonesian people hope that in a very short time our red and white Indonesian flag shall fly bravely in the West Irian sky. May God Almighty give His blessing to our struggle to liberate West Irian on the basis of love for peace and justice and, even more, our great love for the freedom of our country. He, God Almighty, spoke in the Holy Book Koran, verse *Al-mumtahimah,* that He does not prohibit a friendly attitude towards those who are not hostile to you and who act with justice,

But Allah prohibits unto thee, towards those who are hostile to thee . . . and who banish thee from thine homeland, and towards them thou art prohibited to have a friendly attitude.

Yes, let us continue our struggle against colonialism and

imperialism relentlessly. If we do this, if we speed up the eradication of colonialism and help to halt the colonial wars now raging, we shall have done something indeed. But I use the word "something" deliberately, fully conscious that having achieved this we shall not yet have achieved all our aims. In Indonesia I have repeatedly told the people that independence is only a bridge, though a precious golden bridge; a bridge for nation-building, a bridge for national construction, a bridge for winning better living conditions, a bridge for the establishment of social justice. Yes, and I have stressed that national independence is a bridge for the brotherhood of mankind and for eternal peace in the world.

And in international relations, too, independence is a bridge; a bridge for the struggle of nations for emancipation, for the building of nations and states that are able to stand on their own feet, politically, economically and in every other way; a bridge for justice among nations. The creation of national regimes without the concomitant process of emancipation will not further stability, prosperity and justice in the world, quite the contrary. In the past, and even today, we have had many examples of national regimes which make no effort towards emancipation. These regimes are not only a plague to their own peoples, they are a plague to the world, because they easily fall prey to foreign intervention, become the playground of rivalries between foreign powers, the battlefield for foreign powers in their struggle for domination. These regimes become the source of international conflict.

There can be no alternative for us. Just as we have persistently waged the struggle for liberation against colonialism and are still doing so today, so must we, just as persistently, struggle for international emancipation. It is only through the simultaneous struggle for liberation and emancipation that we can advance towards the new international order of stable and independent states, a lasting international order, one which can withstand the shock of even the most radical technical advances. However stormy it may be this march towards the new order of world justice is far safer than preserving the old world of silent colonization and exploitation.

The problem of emancipation lies at the source of many of the international issues which have been put on the agenda of our conference. The problem of non-intervention and non-interference, the problem of peaceful co-existence, the problem of racial discrimination, and even the problem of the structure of the United Nations—all these are problems which have been thrust onto the scene by the process of emancipation. As a result of this process new social and economic forces have emerged in the world. Socialist countries based on Marxism have emerged; independent countries, big and small, in Asia and Africa have emerged; and side by side with other independent countries they are pressing for national construction and for laying a solid foundation to their nation-building, based on the requirements of our age.

As I have said, these are living realities, realities which cannot be denied. The world must accept them. Perhaps they do not conform to the norms and standards of the past, but they are here, and they are an indispensable part of the emancipation process, indispensable to the march towards a new world order of peace, justice and prosperity. This emergence of non-conformity with the past is reflected in the conflict of ideologies, in the conflict of economic interests, in the conflict of military interests. The fact that conflicts have emerged must not make us abandon non-conformity. On the contrary, we must abandon the old dogmas; the march of history has proved that they are out of tune with a world society of peace, based on equal liberty, justice and a fair share for all.

What, then, is the way to solve burning present-day issues? Where the conflict of the old interest and the emerging forces has become very acute and explosive we must as a first step accept the status quo. As a second step we must accept the principle of peaceful co-existence not only in words but also in deeds. Concrete action must be taken to reduce feelings of hostility by urging the contending parties to initiate talks with the aim of beginning to understand each other. Do not befog the issues by standing stubbornly by previously adopted positions in order to "save face." The aim must be to find an acceptable solution around the negotiating table so as to save the world from extinction.

Let me issue a warning. Miscalculation of the facts as they exist, bluffing in order to see how far the other side will go, may bring us to the verge of disaster. The alternative to peaceful co-existence between the two blocs is war of unimaginable magnitude. True, peaceful co-existence does not immediately restore the position to normal, it does not remove conflicts; but it does remove acute feelings of hostility, and that alone is a gain.

A glance into history provides us with many examples of tolerance prevailing over bigotry and narrow-mindedness, of new ideas and creeds at first condemned as heresy later co-existing with older dogmas. Christianity and Islam today co-exist after centuries of crusade and counter-crusade; Protestantism and Catholicism today co-exist though at first Rome condemned Martin Luther as a heretic and treated him as an outcast. Let us learn from the experiences of our forefathers, learn to avoid their mistakes, their centuries of crusading and bigotry; learn how eventually tolerance prevailed, with different ideologies and creeds living peacefully side by side, each recognizing the rights of the other to live without in any way compromising on principles.

This is why we in Indonesia firmly believe that the ideological conflict is not, I repeat, not the main problem of our time. It is not a problem which affects the majority of mankind, such as poverty, disease, illiteracy and colonial bondage.

But, people may ask, if we adopt the principle of peaceful co-existence, will this mean preserving the status quo forever? My reply is quite definitely no. How can we expect to perpetuate the division of nations? How can we expect to prevent nations from evolving their own national concepts of life based on their own brands of socialism, Marxism or capitalism? How can we prevent nations replacing monarchies by republics, or the reverse, if they wish? No, peaceful co-existence cannot and should not perpetuate the status quo. It must allow every nation to develop as it sees fit, unhampered by external pressures or interference.

Applied to Germany and West Berlin these principles can, I am sure, reduce the acute tensions of today. Formalize or legalize existing conditions; remove all possibility of a spread of hostilities; accept the difference in social outlook; avoid every single act which might provoke greater mistrust and suspicion; withdraw all interference from outside; let the Germans themselves decide their future destiny. Let them initiate talks in a serious endeavor to reach understanding. Let them take initial steps, however small, towards the creation and strengthening of regular forms of contact. Trade is an excellent example of this. After all, the Germans are wise enough to know that international conflict over Germany would obliterate their entire national life, and rearmament will not save them from this fate.

Common sense must prevail. Yes, and common sense demands the recognition of the temporary de facto sovereignty of two Germanies as a big reality. Common sense also demands that West Berlin should not become the playground of big-power conflicts, or ideological conflict. The people of West Berlin should be left to themselves to conduct their lives without interference from outside. The people of West Berlin should have free access to the other parts of the world, and the people of the world should also have free access to West Berlin. This, I think, can be arranged through the recognition of both Germanies as the de facto position of two states. And if the Soviet Union chooses to conclude a peace treaty with East Germany, let it be so. To achieve this, the big powers must come to the negotiating table to end the present crisis, fully conscious of their responsibilities towards the world. The problem of Germany, a nation divided against itself, has too long been a threat to peace in Europe and the world. The non-aligned countries, by proposing principles for its solution such as I have outlined above, can make a major contribution towards preserving world peace at a time when it stands in great danger.

Now I will say something about the United Nations. The rapid march of developments in the past few years—the establishment of new independent states, the role of non-alignment in international affairs, the growing desire for peaceful co-existence, the march of the revolution being waged by three-quarters of mankind—is showing with increasing clarity that the structure of the United Nations needs to be overhauled. The United Nations was set up in 1945. Who can deny that the political map of the world has radically altered since then? Who can deny that the composition of the big powers has altered? Who, for example, can deny that the People's Republic of China exercises authority over the more than 600 million Chinese people?

The United Nations was set up in order to be a stabilizing factor in world affairs. It was set up in order to preserve and consolidate peace. It was set up as an instrument through which the advanced nations could render assistance to other nations to help them overcome poverty and economic and technical backwardness. If it is to do all this— in short, if the United Nations is to play a positive and progressive role in this age of liberation and emancipation— then its structure must reflect the composition of nations that makes up our world community of today. Its failure to do so is a contradiction of reality; it can only create new dissensions and deepen the existing ones.

The United Nations must not be allowed to become the instrument of any power bloc. We know from experience that the United Nations is not functioning properly today. Voting is all too frequently determined not by the merits of the case but by external pressures and considerations in the interests of one set of nations, one power bloc. It is our duty to do all we can to make this world organization a center of world stability, a means of consolidating relations between nations, an instrument for putting the principles of peaceful co-existence into practice. It is our duty to ensure that the new, emergent forces find adequate recognition there and can exert a rightful influence in the world councils where major world problems are considered.

For all these reasons I strongly urge that the United Nations structure requires reorganization. This applies to the membership of the United Nations in general. This applies to the membership of the Security Council, as well as to the composition of the Secretariat and other United Nations bodies.

Another problem on our agenda is the question of disarmament. No one here in this hall disagrees with the need for disarmament. Indeed, people the world over are more and more persistently demanding disarmament. They demand this because history has taught time and time again that the armaments race leads to war. They demand this because rearmament is one of the most effective ways of subjugating other peoples, because rearmament is the road to imperialism. They demand this because disarmament will release tremendous resources for construction and for raising living standards throughout the world.

Apart from the handful of people who stand to gain from the expansion of war industries, no sane person in the world agrees with rearmament. And, too, no single person in the world can escape from the devastation of war and its aftermath.

The rearmaments race is the result of fear and mistrust between the big powers; and similarly the rearmaments race leads to greater fear, greater mistrust. Therefore we believe that the key to success in disarmament rests in first disarming mistrust, disarming fear, disarming men's suspicions of one another. The non-aligned countries must be given an active role—I repeat, an active role—in the task of finding a solution to this complicated problem.

We demand this because the decision as regards peace or war should not be left to the big powers alone. No, the decision on peace or war should not be left mainly to the powers which possess nuclear weapons and missiles. The decision on peace or war is a matter which should be in the hands of all people in the world. This only is the surest way to peace.

I am now coming to the closing remarks of my speech.

For most of us it was not an easy decision to come to this conference. Many problems occupy us at home; we are moving from one urgency to the next in order to keep pace with the process of national advancement. But we came because we knew this conference would be important, that it would take us an important step forward in the noble task of helping to establish and preserve peace based on prosperity, social justice and cooperation among all nations.

This conference is not an isolated event in the emergence of the new social forces. It is one of a series of major events in this process of emergence. The first was the Asian relations conference held in New Delhi in 1948, a conference which in one of its resolutions condemned the military attack by the Dutch on the Republic of Indonesia. That conference was a protest against colonialism in its purest form.

The next major conference, and one whose echoes are still reverberating around the world, was the Asian-African conference held in Bandung, Indonesia, in April, 1955. The purpose of that conference was to cement and consolidate the cooperation between the independent peoples of Asia and Africa in their struggle for a just and prosperous society and the continuation of the struggle of the colonial peoples against imperialism and colonialism in all its forms. Then we had the regional conferences of our African sister nations.

And now we have this present conference, the basic purpose of which is to draw the non-aligned countries into a coordinated accumulated moral force in order to help preserve world peace and bring about a new stable equilibrium based on a world order of social justice and prosperity.

I have already explained that such an order is not possible without the eradication of colonialism and imperialism in the world. So our purpose here is also to contribute relentlessly to the struggle against the remnants of colonialism and imperialism. And so our conference is not a rival to the Asian-African conference but must be complementary to it. The conference of non-aligned nations must be a joining brother to Asian-African solidarity, it must contribute strength to it. Our conference today and the Asian-African conference are two comrades in arms. If we want to make dynamic progress in the struggle for liberation, emancipation and world stability I hope that this conference will bear in mind the necessity for a second Asian-African conference in the near future.

I deem it necessary also to express my hope that at the end of this conference the international world will appreciate the compactness and dynamic unity inherent in all decisions of the Belgrade convention. For this purpose I hope that the conference will be able to accept a charter of statements by our convention in Belgrade. This charter will embrace all decisions we take.

The existence of such a charter of statements will certainly facilitate the forwarding of the decisions of the convention directly to the forthcoming General Assembly of the United Nations, so that the benefits of the results of this conference, as a complementary body to the Asian-African conference, can immediately be utilized by the members of the United Nations. It is up to the Belgrade conference to determine the composition of the mission which is to present the charter of statements to the General Assembly of the United Nations in 1961.

Yes, let us bear in mind that our purpose here is to contribute relentlessly to the struggle against the remnants of colonialism and imperialism; to make a collective contribution towards easing international tensions; to coordinate our efforts to facilitate the process of emancipation between nations; not only to build new nationhoods but also to build a new world—to build the world anew.

Yes, our task is to build the world anew, there is no alternative to that. The conviction that this is so must spur us on to even greater efforts, until our struggle has been crowned with success. Through the years our task as independent nations has expanded, and we cannot escape these responsibilities.

We live in a terrifically dynamic time, a time full of dangers. The occasion is piled high with difficulties, but we may not flee from those difficulties, we must rise to the occasion. But the dogmas of the quiet past are inadequate to the stormy present. As our case is new, we must think anew, we must act anew, we must shape anew, we must re-shape anew. We must disenthrall ourselves. Only when we do so can this conference of high expectations bear fruit.

May the Almighty bless and guide us all.

Bismillah.

ADDRESS BY
PRIME MINISTER
JAWAHARLAL NEHRU OF INDIA

Standing here before this distinguished assembly, I feel moved. I think of the past decades and I see many faces of old comrades and friends who devoted most of their life in the struggle for freedom, and many of them succeeded and many of them have passed away. I see younger faces too, representing their peoples, heads of newly free countries, and I see this great movement of freedom from colonial domination, led by many of the distinguished delegates here, going forward and meeting with success, indeed proving that, in so far as any historical perspective is concerned, the era of classic colonialism is gone and is dead, though of course it survives and gives a lot of trouble yet; but essentially it is over.

I think it was a happy and wise thought of the sponsors of this conference to have convened it, and it has turned out to be an even happier thought because of subsequent developments. I am glad that we are meeting here in this pleasant and friendly city of Belgrade and more specially under the auspices of the government and especially the leader, President Tito, of this government and its people.

I said that it has become an even more important thing that we meet today; it would have been important in any event but it has become more important because of the developments of the last two or three months, when strange things have happened in the world and have suddenly drawn our attention to the abyss stretching out before us and below us. I think that the attention that this conference has attracted in the world, it would have attracted anyhow; but that attention is much more today because we meet at this particular crisis in human destiny.

People all over the world are vastly interested to know what we think about this crisis, where our thoughts or actions are going to lead us, what advice we give, what pressure we may exercise in solving this crisis. It is well to remember this because today everything that we have contended against and that we are continuing to struggle against—imperialism, colonialism, racialism and the rest—things which are very important and to which reference has been made repeatedly here, all these things are somewhat overshadowed by this crisis. For if war comes all else for the moment goes. Therefore it becomes inevitable for us to pay attention to, and not only to pay attention to but to make sure that the dominant note of our thinking and action and what we say and put down is this crisis that confronts humanity. People expect us to do this. The great powers even also watch us and listen to us, and are watching for what we shall do, and I am quite sure that vast numbers of individuals in every country are thinking of this more even than of the normal subjects that rightly occupy our attention.

We call ourselves a conference of non-aligned countries. Now, the word "non-aligned" may be differently interpreted but basically it was used, and coined almost, with the meaning non-aligned with the great power blocs of the world. Non-aligned has a negative meaning, but if you give it a positive connotation it means nations which object to this lining-up for war purposes—military blocs, military alliances and the like. Therefore we keep away from this and we want to throw our weight, such as it is, in favor of peace. In effect, therefore, when there is a crisis involving the possibility of war, the very fact that we are unaligned should stir us to action, should stir us to thought, should stir us to feel that now more than ever it is up to us to do whatever we can to prevent such a calamity coming down upon us. So from every point of view and from the point of view of our inception and being as modern nations this problem is dominantly before us. I want to lay stress on this because, since we are engaged with many other difficult problems, which face us as a whole, which face us as individual countries, for all of us have problems, it is a little dangerous with this particular crisis that we might really put this major problem in the background. I repeat, I say so with all respect for all the other problems we have before us. That, I think, would be little short of tragedy because we would have failed in our purpose, we would have failed to meet the demands made by humanity on us today when it is facing this crisis. And they will say: "Yes, what they say is good, we agree, but how does it save us now, today, from the crisis that is the immediate problem? If this does not save us and war comes, what good will their long speeches and declaration have done?" That will be the answer of humanity.

I therefore submit that we must look at things in the proper perspective today. First things must come first, and nothing is more important or has more priority than this world situation of war and peace. Everything else, however vital to us—and other things are vital to us—has a secondary place. If, in this crisis, something we do, some action of ours or some words of ours, helps to some extent to resolve the problem, to remove the fear of war, then we have justified ourselves and strengthened ourselves in order to meet all the other problems that face us. On the other hand, if we cannot face this matter straightforwardly and clearly in our own minds then somehow we fail mankind in this crisis, we give no lead. Of course we stand for anti-colonialism, anti-imperialism, anti-racialism and all that. All our lives, the lives of most of us present here, have been spent in that and we shall continue the struggle, but nevertheless the point arises, at this particular crisis, as to what we are going to do. Pass long resolutions and make brave declarations? That is easy enough; we have done it before and we can do it today too; but what else can we do to meet the crisis, because the problem of war and peace has an intimate relation to all those other matters we stand for. It is war or the fear of war that has led to the cold war. It is the cold war which has resulted and is resulting in the old imperialism and the old colonialism hanging on wherever they exist because they deem it advantageous.

So what I wish with all respect to place before this assembly is this: That we must make first things first, and the first thing today is this fear of war, because ever since the last war there have been many ups and downs, many crises, many dangerous situations that have come up. We have got over them somehow or other, but the present situation is by far the most dangerous that has arisen in the last fifteen years or so since the last war ended.

It has become a commonplace for people in every country to refer to the dangers of modern nuclear warfare. Although we talk about it, I am not so sure that even those who talk about it fully and emotionally realize what this means. We talk about the destruction of civilization, the destruction of humanity, the destruction of the human race, if nuclear war comes. Well, if this is so, something much more is required, some greater effort, some greater attempt on our part to do what we can to avoid it. I know that the key to the situation does not lie in the hands of this conference or in those of other congresses or conferences. The key to the situation today lies essentially in the hands of two great powers—the United States of America and the Soviet Union. Nevertheless I think that this conference, or rather the countries that are represented in this conference, are not so helpless that they can look on while the world is destroyed and war is declared. I think we can make a difference —possibly we can, I cannot guarantee it—and if so we should try our utmost to do it and not talk about other subjects, even though they are important subjects, while the world goes to its doom. That is the thing I would beg this assembly to remember. And I would beg that, in whatever declaration it may make, this should be put foremost and topmost, and perhaps be isolated to show that it is the main thing, that other things may be very important but they are secondary. If this is done it will undoubtedly create a far greater impression than would a mere record of the various other problems that face us, although they are very important problems. I do not deny this, and we should act accordingly, but there is a time and a place to press any subject and today the time and the place and the occasion are here to take up this question of war and peace and make it our own and show the world that we stand for peace and that, so far as we can, we shall fight for it—not fight in the sense of guns, but struggle for it in the ways open to us.

I would like to lay stress on this right at the beginning of the few words that I wish to say to this assembly, because while on the one hand I see the power of the nations assembled here—which is not military power, which is not economic power, but which nevertheless is a power; call it moral force, call it what you will, it does make a difference, obviously, what we in our combined wisdom feel and think and what we are prepared to do—on the other hand, a fear creeps in upon my mind that we may not be able to get out of the rut of meeting together, passing long resolutions and making brave declarations, and then going home and allowing the world to drift to disaster. That itself will be a tragedy when so much is expected by our people, the people whom we represent here, and indeed by so many people outside in other countries who may not be represented here but who are looking up to us.

It is a strange thing that some few years ago—six, seven or eight, if you like—this business of non-alignment was a rare phenomenon. A few countries here and there talked about it and other countries rather made fun of it, or at any rate did not take it seriously. "Non-alignment? What is this? You must be on this side or that side." That was the argument. Well, that argument is dead today; nobody dares say that, because the whole course of history of the last few years has shown the growing opinion, the spread of this conception of non-alignment. Why is that so? Because it was in tune with the course of events; it was in tune with the thinking of vast numbers of people, whether the country concerned was non-aligned or not; it was in tune with it because they hungered passionately for peace and did not like this massing up of vast armies and nuclear bombs on either side. Therefore their minds turned to those countries who refused to line up with these people.

Maybe some of us did not approach this question with blank minds, this question of war and peace and whatever lies behind this cold war. We had our opinions, we had our inclinations, but essentially we were against this business of a cold war and all that it implied, and the massing up of weapons and bombs, etc. We talked, everybody talked, and still talks about disarmament. As my friend and colleague President Nkrumah has said, disarmament is a most vital thing. I entirely agree with him. The fact is that while we have talked about disarmament the world has gone on arming more and more.

What does all this mean? There is something wrong, some gap between our thinking and the action the world takes. The basic fact is that the world which has talked of disarmament month after month, year after year, has been arming more and more, and it has arrived almost at the final stage when either it disarms or it bursts. There is no choice left today, and in this field of maneuvering the choice is getting more and more limited. When each party digs in its toes to particular positions, when each great country, even smaller countries, feel their national honor is involved it is difficult to move them. When big countries feel that their national honor is involved they risk war, whatever the consequences. That is what we are getting to. It is possible when these rigid attitudes are taken that an indication from this conference and all those whom it represents—they are many and they count, in great parts of the world—a positive indication might have some slight effect on these great protagonists who, with their nuclear bombs, threaten each other, and incidentally threaten all of us, because it is now known very well that the effects of war will not be confined to those great powers or their lives, but other countries which are not in the war will also suffer. Presumably if war comes the countries represented here will not rush into the war; they will remain apart. But what good will it do them to remain apart when they will suffer from it, and when the whole world will suffer?

Therefore, we have arrived at the position today where there is no choice. Well, to say there is no choice between war and peace sounds rather fatuous. I put it this way: There is no choice left between an attempt, between negotiations for peace or war. If people refuse to negotiate they must inevitably go to war. There is no choice. They must negotiate, and I am amazed and surprised that rigid, proud attitudes are taken up by great countries, all being too high and mighty to negotiate for peace. I submit with all humility to them and to others that this is not a right attitude, because it is not their pride that is involved in it but the future of the human race.

I cannot—and I rather doubt if even this assembly can —go into these matters and suggest, "You must negotiate on these lines," or "You must come to terms on these lines." I do not think that is possible for us, or suitable. We may have our ideas, and when the time comes we may even say so, but our indicating "These are the lines for your settlement, for negotiation" instead of helping may hinder, because we are dealing with proud nations and they may react wrongly. Therefore, we cannot really lay down any terms on which they should negotiate. But it is our duty and function to say that they must negotiate, and any party that does not do so does tremendous injury to the human race.

I am not talking about basic agreements between rival ideas, rival ideologies and rival attempts to increase the power of a nation. I do not think that by one stroke you can solve all these problems, or that anybody can. But at the present juncture one has to see how to lessen these tensions, how at least to remove some of the obstructions to peace, how at least to prevent war coming. If that is done, then other steps will naturally follow.

I believe firmly that the only possible way ultimately to solve these problems, or many of them, is by complete disarmament. Yet it would be absurd for me to say, "In the next week or month, decide on complete disarmament" because it is not a practicable proposition. Today the situation is such that their fears from each other are leading them towards greater armaments all the time, whether you look at one side or the other. Therefore, although I consider disarmament an absolute necessity for the peace of the world in the future—I think that without disarmament these difficulties, fears and conflicts will continue—nevertheless one cannot expect suddenly, because this conference wants it, disarmament to appear on the scene in full panoply. We should lay stress on disarmament, of course, but for the present moment the only thing that we can do is to lay stress on the fact of negotiations with a view to getting over these present fears and dangers. If that is done, the next and third step follows and may be taken.

I would venture to say that it is not for us even to lay down what should be done in regard to Germany or Berlin, which are the immediate causes of this present tension. There are some things that seem to me obvious. For instance —and others have referred to it too—it seems to me obvious that certain facts of life should be recognized. The facts of life are, first, that there are two independent entities, powers, countries: the Government of Western Germany (the Federal Republic of Germany) and the Government of Eastern Germany (the German Democratic People's Republic). That is a fact of life: It is not a matter of my or anyone else's liking or disliking it; it is a fact that has to be recognized. If you ignore the facts of life and the facts of contemporary politics that means that you are ignoring something which will lead you to wrong results.

The second thing (I am expressing my own opinion for the moment) is that as things are we find this great city of Berlin divided by what might be called an international frontier. It is a very awkward situation, but there it is. But anyhow West Berlin is very closely allied to Western Germany, to the Western countries, and they have had these routes of access to them, and I am glad that Mr. Khrushchev himself has indicated that that access will not be limited; it will be open to them as it is now. Now if that is made perfectly clear and guaranteed by all concerned I should imagine that one of the major fears and major causes of conflict will be removed.

I am merely putting this forward to indicate how some of the big things that are troubling people are capable of solution without solving the entire problem. If some things are understood and agreed to definitely, immediately, the fear of war in the near future disappears. Other things can be considered later. So I venture to say that the most important thing for the world today is for these great powers directly concerned to meet together and negotiate with the will to peace, and not to stand too much on their respective prestige; and I think that if this conference throws its weight on that, as I am sure it must be prepared to do, it will be a positive step which we take to help.

Take again the United Nations. As far as I remember, when the United Nations was formed one of its early articles said it was formed to save succeeding generations from the scourge of war. That was the main purpose of the United Nations—to save humanity from the scourge of war.

Here is a situation arising which threatens war very definitely. What will the United Nations do about it?

I remember I was in Geneva in 1938, in the summer or the autumn, and the old League of Nations was meeting there when the whole of Europe was tense with fear of war. War came a year later, but even in 1938 it was tense because Hitler was marching this way and that way all over Europe. He went to Czechoslovakia and held it and he went to some other place, advancing all the time. There was this fear of war lying all over Europe, but the League of Nations in Geneva was discussing at that time, I think, the opium traffic. Very important, the opium traffic, undoubtedly; but something else was more important than the opium traffic, and that was war. And war came a year later. It was postponed only: It came in 1939.

Now I do not want the United Nations to function as the League of Nations did. I do not think it will, but I merely mention this. What can the United Nations do? The whole framework of the United Nations, ever since it was formed fifteen years ago, was the recognition of the balance of power in the world. That is why they had certain permanent members in the Security Council, vetoing, etc.—all that business. Now of course the world has changed since then, considerably, and there are many more members and this requires a change in the structure, etc., of the United Nations. That is true. Nevertheless the United Nations cannot easily ignore the balance of power in the world. It has to keep that in view. Anyhow, the point is that it is the duty of the United Nations to consider this matter and try its utmost to solve it.

The United Nations meets from time to time for special causes, special discussions. I would have suggested, if it was not meeting as it it, I think, in about two weeks' time (or less), its meeting quickly to consider these matters. I am not suggesting the United Nations should sit down and consider Germany, Berlin and all that. No. I say it should meet to consider a situation which might lead to war and take such steps, in its united wisdom, as it can. Fortunately it is meeting. I should say one of the earliest things it should do is to deal with this problem. All other problems are secondary: It should postpone them, or put them lower down on its agenda.

Now I feel strongly that this matter requires our urgent attention and the urgent attention of every government and every organization in the world. Since it so happens by accident—or that circumstances have so dealt with us—that we in this conference are meeting at this time of grave crisis, we should seize hold of it in so far as we can. I recognize that we cannot issue mandates. I think we are an important conference. I think we represent countries which individually, and certainly jointly, represent something important and valuable in the world and our voice counts to some extent. That is true.

At the same time we must not overestimate our own importance. After all, we do not control the strings of the world, not only in the military sense but in other senses also. If our mandate ran it would be easy enough—we would issue the mandate. But we know that our mandate does not run all over the place. So we must realize that. We must realize both our actual and our potential strength that we have, and also the lack of strength that we have. Both have to be considered together, then we should decide what to do.

So I am venturing to suggest not any specific course of action but rather a mental outlook that should govern us in approaching this problem: That we should think of this as the most vital and important problem of the day and everything else as being secondary, however important it is. We can deal with other things more effectively and more strongly after we have dealt with this. Otherwise no other problems remain: They are submerged in the terrible disaster of war.

That is the main point I should like to place before this assembly.

Now, sir, may I add here that this danger of war comes nearer and nearer, has been enhanced and has become nearer to us, perhaps, by the recent decision of the Soviet government to start nuclear tests. Now I am not in a position, and I suppose no one else here is in a position, to know all the facts which underlie these decisions—all the military considerations, political, non-political considerations, whatever they may be—but one thing I know: That this decision makes the situation much more dangerous. That is obvious to me; therefore I regret it deeply because it may well lead to other countries also starting this and then, apart from the danger inherent in nuclear tests—that is, radioactive substances falling and all that—all this brings us to the very verge and precipice of war. That is why I deeply regret it, and because of all this it has become even more urgent that this process of negotiation should begin without any delay, without thinking of who is going to ask whom first. The person who asks first will deserve credit, not the person who shrinks from asking others.

I should just like to refer, briefly, I hope, to some of our other problems. Many of the countries represented here have only recently become free or independent. They have tremendous problems and, above all, the problem of making good and to advance their own people, economically, socially, etc., because we must recognize that most of these countries are underdeveloped—nearly all. We must recognize that they are socially and economically backward countries, and it is not an easy matter to get rid of this inheritance of backwardness and underdevelopment. It requires clear thinking. It requires action. It requires a tremendous amount of hard work, and all of us have to face that. I think that it is right and proper that other countries, the affluent countries, the rich countries, should help in this process. They should do it. They have to some extent done it. I think they should do more of it, but whatever they may do the ultimate burden will lie on the people of our own countries. If it did not, if by some miracle or somebody else's help we stood up, well we would fall down again. When you stand up, you do not stand long when you do not have the strength. The ultimate burden is on us. So it is no good expecting others to do all of our work.

Therefore, this great problem faces each one of our countries, and in facing it we have to think of this modern world which has not only changed greatly but which is changing from day to day: this world of atomic energy and jet and space travel, new forces being let loose and the tremendous value and importance of science today. We have to think of that. We cannot just imitate somebody else and put a little machine here, a machine there, and think we are making progress. We have to catch up with the modern world and with science and technology, keeping our own values intact, I hope.

All these problems can overwhelm us. Why I am venturing to refer to obvious things is that really in considering our other problems we may keep these basic things in view.

There are other countries, some represented here; others whom we know very well which are struggling for their freedom from grasping colonialism or imperialism which will not go. There is Algeria, which has paid a fantastic price in human life and suffering in its struggle for freedom and yet which has not so far succeeded in achieving it. Naturally, everyone present here is wholly desirous of Algeria becoming independent, and I earnestly hope that this will be so.

There is Tunisia, with its recent extraordinary experience, and I am referring particularly to Bizerta. Why Bizerta? Because Bizerta is a foreign base, and the very idea of a foreign base in a country seems quite extraordinary to me. It is bad enough to have bases anyway, but that a country should put its foreign base in another country seems quite extraordinary to me. How can that be tolerated by anybody? I do not understand how anyone can provide for a base in a country which opposes that base, purely from the practical point of view.

There are these problems of Africa, the Congo, and may I say I am glad to learn that possibly by tomorrow we shall have here in this assembly the Prime Minister and the Deputy Prime Minister of the Congo Republic, Mr. Adoula and Mr. Gizenga. There is Angola, the horror of Angola. I do not know how many of the delegates present here have had occasion to read the detailed accounts of what has happened in Angola, because Angola has been a closed book. But something is happening in Angola—not only in Angola but round about—which really has a kind of horror which one hardly associates with the modern world—massacres, genocide, and so on. Of course, our minds go out, and we need not only to sympathize; we want to do what we can to put an end to this. Yet we cannot do very much as a rule, although sometimes we may do a little. All these problems face us.

Then there is the situation in East Africa, where conditions are better, of course, and to some extent some countries have been promised independence, such as Tanganyika, I believe, by December, and other countries I hope also. There is the situation in Central Africa—the Rhodesias —where the picture is not good; there is trouble. And further south, in South Africa, you have the supreme symbol of racial arrogance, racial discrimination, apartheid and all that, which is an intolerable position to be accepted by any of us. And this is imposed upon South-West Africa, in challenge to the United Nations decisions. So all these problems crowd upon us and we have to face them, of course.

For the moment, however, I would repeat that whatever we may do about the other problems—and we should do whatever we can—the problem dominating the issue today is that of this danger of war. The danger of war depends on many factors, but essentially on two major countries, the United States of America and the Soviet Union. It will do us no good, I think, if we start condemning this country or that country. It is not a very easy thing to do anyhow; it has a complicated set of circumstances. But apart from being easy or difficult, if we are to be peacemakers and if we want to help in the cause of peace, it does not help to start by condemnations. We want to win over and to influence and induce them to follow the path of peace, and if we denounce the countries then we cannot influence them, whatever else we can do. We cannot win them over. The times demand, therefore, that we should approach these countries and other countries in a friendly way, in a wa, to win them over and not merely to denounce them and irritate them and make it even more difficult for them to follow the path we indicate to them.

Let us look at this world today. It is a strange world, perhaps the most fundamental fact of the world being the coming out of these new mighty forces. I am referring to atomic energy, space travel and all that, which is the basic factor of the modern world. We have to think in terms of that, and not get lost in the terms of a world which is past and in slogans that no longer apply. But this is the world that we live in. When power of a new kind comes, all your imperialism and all your old-style colonialism will vanish and will go, I have no doubt. And yet this new power may well dominate over us and dominate certainly the underdeveloped backward countries, because the sin of backwardness has to pay the penalty by somebody pushing you about. We cannot afford to be backward, therefore we have to build in our own countries societies of free men, societies where freedom is real—because I do think freedom is essential, that freedom will give us strength—prosperous societies where the standards of living are rising. These are for us the essential, basic problems to be thought out in terms of today, in terms of the modern world, space travel, jet travel, atomic energy, not in terms of long ago. When you think in these terms war becomes an even greater folly and anachronism than ever. If we cannot prevent war then for the moment all our other problems are sunk, we cannot deal with them. But if we can prevent war we can go ahead on our other problems, help to liberate parts of the world under colonial and other imperial rule, and more especially build up our own free societies, prosperous societies, welfare states, in our respective countries, because that is to be our positive work. Merely getting angry with some other country achieves nothing, although one does get angry and cannot help it. It is the positive constructive work we do that gives us strength to make our countries free. That is the positive work we have to do.

But we cannot do any of this unless there is no war. If war comes all is doomed. Therefore I venture to submit to this assembly that we must lay the greatest stress on this major danger of today. Not only is this incumbent on us but if we do this we shall be in line with the thinking of millions and millions of people. Strength comes ultimately from being in line with popular thinking. The fact that we are non-aligned has received strength from the fact that millions of people are not aligned, they do not want war, that is why we get indirect strength from this. Today this is the problem of practically the entire population of the world. Let us put ourselves in line with it and deal with it as well as we can, realizing fully of course that our capacity is limited. We must not imagine that we can order about great countries or as small countries do as we like. Our capacity is limited, but we have a certain capacity, a certain strength, call it what you like, moral strength, or other strength. Let us use it properly, rightly, without force but with courtesy and with a friendly approach so that we may influence those who have the power of war and peace in their hands, and thus try if not to prevent war for all time at any rate to push it away so that in the meantime the world may learn the better use of cooperation. Then ultimately the world may put an end to war itself.

I will repeat that I think that essentially we can never succeed unless there is disarmament on the biggest scale. Therefore disarmament is a vital matter, but even that is rather out of reach today, because how can we talk of disarmament when we are told that we are going to have nuclear tests today and tomorrow, and when we are told that all these great countries are becoming more and more heavily armed?

I have ventured to express some of the ideas in my mind. I have not dealt with the various items on the agenda because I feel that the first item overshadows all else. The others should be dealt with no doubt and I hope that when this matter comes up and some kind of resolution or declaration or statement is being issued attention will be paid to this question of world peace being put not only foremost but so that it catches every person's attention and so that it does not get lost in a morass of detail and thus lose all significance and importance.

DECLARATION OF THE HEADS OF STATE OR GOVERNMENT OF NON-ALIGNED COUNTRIES

The conference of heads of state or government of the following non-aligned countries:

1. Afghanistan	13. Indonesia
2. Algeria	14. Iraq
3. Burma	15. Lebanon
4. Cambodia	16. Mali
5. Ceylon	17. Morocco
6. Congo	18. Nepal
7. Cuba	19. Saudi Arabia
8. Cyprus	20. Somalia
9. Ethiopia	21. Sudan
10. Ghana	22. Tunisia
11. Guinea	23. United Arab Republic
12. India	24. Yemen
	25. Yugoslavia

and of the following countries represented by observers:

1. Bolivia   2. Brazil   3. Ecuador

was held in Belgrade from September 1 to 6, 1961, for the purpose of exchanging views on international problems with a view to contributing more effectively to world peace and security and peaceful cooperation among peoples.

The heads of state or government of the aforementioned countries have met at a moment when international events have taken a turn for the worst and when world peace is seriously threatened. Deeply concerned for the future of

peace, voicing the aspirations of the vast majority of people
of the world, aware that, in our time, no people and no
government can or should abandon its responsibilities in
regard to the safeguarding of world peace, the participating
countries—having examined in detail, in an atmosphere of
equality, sincerity and mutual confidence, the current state
of international relations and trends prevailing in the present-day world—make the following declaration:

The heads of state or government of non-aligned countries noting that there are crises that lead towards a world
conflict in the transition from an old order based on domination to a new order based on cooperation between nations,
founded on freedom, equality and social justice for the
promotion of prosperity; considering that the dynamic processes and forms of social change often result in or represent
a conflict between the old established and the new emerging
nationalist forces; considering that a lasting peace can be
achieved only if this confrontation leads to a world where
the domination of colonialism-imperialism and neo-colonialism in all their manifestations is radically eliminated;

and recognizing the fact that acute emergencies threatening world peace now exist in this period of conflict in
Africa, Asia, Europe and Latin America and big power
rivalry likely to result in world conflagration cannot be
excluded;

that to eradicate basically the source of conflict is to
eradicate colonialism in all its manifestations and to accept
and practice a policy of peaceful co-existence in the world;

that guided by these principles the period of transition
and conflict can lay a firm foundation of cooperation and
brotherhood between nations, state the following:

I

War has never threatened mankind with graver consequences than today. On the other hand, never before has

mankind had at its disposal stronger forces for eliminating war as an instrument of policy in international relations.

Imperialism is weakening. Colonial empires and other forms of foreign oppression of peoples in Asia, Africa and Latin America are gradually disappearing from the stage of history. Great successes have been achieved in the struggle of many peoples for national independence and equality. In the same way, the peoples of Latin America are continuing to make an increasingly effective contribution to the improvement of international relations. Great social changes in the world are further promoting such a development. All this not only accelerates the end of the epoch of foreign oppression of peoples, but also makes peaceful cooperation among peoples, based on the principles of independence and equal rights, an essential condition for their freedom and progress.

Tremendous progress has been achieved in the development of science, techniques and in the means of economic development.

Prompted by such developments in the world, the vast majority of people are becoming increasingly conscious of the fact that war between peoples constitutes not only an anachronism but also a crime against humanity. This awareness of peoples is becoming a great moral force, capable of exercising a vital influence on the development of international relations.

Relying on this and on the will of their peoples, the governments of countries participating in the conference resolutely reject the view that war, including the cold war, is inevitable, as this view reflects a sense both of helplessness and hopelessness and is contrary to the progress of the world. They affirm their unwavering faith that the international community is able to organize its life without resorting to means which actually belong to a past epoch of human history.

However, the existing military blocs, which are growing into more and more powerful military, economic and political groupings, which, by the logic and nature of their mutual relations, necessarily provoke periodic aggravations of international relations, the cold war and the constant and acute danger of its being transformed into actual war, have become a part of the situation prevailing in international relations.

For all these reasons, the heads of state or government of non-aligned countries wish, in this way, to draw the attention of the world community to the existing situation and to the necessity that all peoples should exert efforts to find a sure road towards the stabilization of peace.

II

The present-day world is characterized by the existence of different social systems. The participating countries do not consider that these differences constitute an insurmountable obstacle for the stabilization of peace, provided attempts at domination and interference in the internal development of other peoples and nations are ruled out.

All peoples and nations have to solve the problems of their own political, economic, social and cultural systems in accordance with their own conditions, needs and potentialities.

Furthermore, any attempt at imposing upon peoples one social or political system or another by force and from outside is a direct threat to world peace.

The participating countries consider that under such conditions the principles of peaceful co-existence are the only alternative to the cold war and to a possible general nuclear catastrophe. Therefore, these principles—which include the right of peoples to self-determination, to independence and to the free determination of the forms and methods of economic, social and cultural development—must be the only basis of all international relations.

Active international cooperation in the fields of material

and cultural exchanges among peoples is an essential means for the strengthening of confidence in the possibility of peaceful co-existence among states with different social systems.

The participants in the conference emphasize, in this connection, that the policy of co-existence amounts to an active effort towards the elimination of historical injustices and the liquidation of national oppression, guaranteeing, at the same time, to every people their independent development.

Aware that ideological differences are necessarily a part of the growth of the human society, the participating countries consider that peoples and governments shall refrain from any use of ideologies for the purpose of waging cold war, exercising pressure, or imposing their will.

III

The heads of state or government of non-aligned countries participating in the conference are not making concrete proposals for the solution of all international disputes, and particularly disputes between the two blocs. They wish, above all, to draw attention to those acute problems of our time which must be solved rapidly, so that they should not lead to irreparable consequences.

In this respect, they particularly emphasize the need for a great sense of responsibility and realism when undertaking the solution of various problems resulting from differences in social systems.

The non-aligned countries represented at this conference do not wish to form a new bloc and cannot be a bloc. They sincerely desire to cooperate with any government which seeks to contribute to the strengthening of confidence and peace in the world.

The non-aligned countries wish to proceed in this manner all the more so as they are aware that peace and stability in the world depend, to a considerable extent, on the mutual relations of the great powers.

Aware of this, the participants in the conference consider it a matter of principle that the great powers take more determined action for the solving of various problems by means of negotiations, displaying at the same time the necessary constructive approach and readiness for reaching solutions which will be mutually acceptable and useful for world peace.

The participants in the conference consider that, under present conditions, the existence and the activities of non-aligned countries in the interests of peace are one of the more important factors for safeguarding world peace.

The participants in the conference consider it essential that the non-aligned countries should participate in solving outstanding international issues concerning peace and security in the world as none of them can remain unaffected by or indifferent to these issues.

They consider that the further extensions of the non-committed area of the world constitutes the only possible and indispensable alternative to the policy of total division of the world into blocs, and intensification of cold war policies. The non-aligned countries provide encouragement and support to all peoples fighting for their independence and equality.

The participants in the conference are convinced that the emergence of newly liberated countries will further assist in narrowing of the area of bloc antagonisms and thus encourage all tendencies aimed at strengthening peace and promoting peaceful cooperation among independent and equal nations.

1. The participants in the conference solemnly reaffirm their support for the "Declaration of the Granting of Independence to Colonial Countries and Peoples," adopted at the fifteenth session of the General Assembly of the United Nations and recommend the immediate unconditional, total

and final abolition of colonialism and resolve to make a concerted effort to put an end to all types of new colonialism and imperialist domination in all its forms and manifestations.

2. The participants in the conference demand that an immediate stop be put to armed action and repressive measures of any kind directed against dependent peoples to enable them to exercise peacefully and freely their right to complete independence and that the integrity of their national territory should be respected. Any aid given by any country to a colonial power in such suppression is contrary to the Charter of the United Nations.

The participating countries, respecting scrupulously the territorial integrity of all states, oppose by all means any aims of annexation by other nations.

3. The participating countries consider the struggle of the people of Algeria for freedom, self-determination and independence, and for the integrity of its national territory including the Sahara, to be just and necessary and are, therefore, determined to extend to the people of Algeria all possible support and aid. The heads of state or government are particularly gratified that Algeria is represented at this conference by its rightful representative, the Prime Minister of the Provisional Government of Algeria.

4. The participating countries draw attention with great concern to the developments in Angola and to the intolerable measures of repression taken by the Portuguese colonial authorities against the people of Angola and demand that an immediate end should be put to any further shedding of blood of the Angolan people, and the people of Angola should be assisted by all peace-loving countries, particularly member states of the United Nations, to establish their free and independent state without delay.

5. The participants in the conference demand the immediate termination of all colonial occupation and the restoration of the territorial integrity to the rightful people in

countries in which it has been violated in Asia, Africa and Latin America as well as the withdrawal of foreign forces from their national soil.

6. The participating countries demand the immediate evacuation of French armed forces from the whole of the Tunisian territory in accordance with the legitimate right of Tunisia to the exercise of its full national sovereignty.

7. The participating countries demand that the tragic events in the Congo must not be repeated and they feel that it is the duty of the world community to continue to do everything in its power in order to erase the consequences and to prevent any further foreign intervention in this young African state, and to enable the Congo to embark freely upon the road of its independent development based on respect for its sovereignty, unity and its territorial integrity.

8. The participants in the conference resolutely condemn the policy of apartheid practiced by the Union of South Africa and demand the immediate abandonment of this policy. They further state that the policy of racial discrimination anywhere in the world constitutes a grave violation of the Charter of the United Nations and the Universal Declaration of Human Rights.

9. The participating countries declare solemnly the absolute respect of the rights of ethnic or religious minorities to be protected in particular against crimes of genocide or any other violation of their fundamental human rights.

10. The participants in the conference condemn the imperialist policies pursued in the Middle East, and declare their support for the full restoration of all the rights of the Arab people of Palestine in conformity with the Charter and resolutions of the United Nations.

11. The participating countries consider the establishment and maintenance of foreign military bases in the territories of other countries, particularly against their express will, a gross violation of the sovereignty of such states. They

declare their full support to countries who are endeavoring to secure the vacation of these bases. They call upon those countries maintaining foreign bases to consider seriously their abolition as a contribution to world peace.

12. They also acknowledge that the North American military base at Guantanamo, Cuba, to the permanence of which the government and people of Cuba have expressed their opposition, affects the sovereignty and territorial integrity of that country.

13. The participants in the conference reaffirm their conviction that:

(a) All nations have the rights of unity, self-determination and independence by virtue of which rights they can determine their political status and freely pursue their economic, social and cultural development without intimidation or hindrance.

(b) All peoples may, for their own ends, freely dispose of their natural wealth and resources without prejudice to any obligations arising out of international economic cooperation, based upon the principle of mutual benefit, and international law. In no case may a people be deprived of its own means of subsistence.

The participating countries believe that the right of Cuba as that of any other nation to freely choose their political and social systems in accordance with their own conditions, needs and possibilities should be respected.

14. The participating countries express their determination that no intimidation, interference or intervention should be brought to bear in the exercise of the right of self-determination of peoples, including their right to pursue constructive and independent policies for the attainment and preservation of their sovereignty.

15. The participants in the conference consider that disarmament is an imperative need and the most urgent task of mankind. A radical solution of this problem, which has become an urgent necessity in the present state of arma-

ments, in the unanimous view of participating countries, can be achieved only by means of a general, complete and strictly and internationally controlled disarmament.

16. The heads of state or government point out that general and complete disarmament should include the elimination of armed forces, armaments, foreign bases, manufacture of arms as well as elimination of institutions and installations for military training, except for purposes of internal security; and the total prohibition of the production, possession and utilization of nuclear and thermo-nuclear arms, bacteriological and chemical weapons as well as the elimination of equipment and installations for the delivery and placement and operational use of weapons of mass destruction on national territories.

17. The participating countries call upon states in general, and states exploring outer space at present in particular, to undertake to use outer space exclusively for peaceful purposes. They express the hope that the international community will, through collective action, establish an international agency with a view to promote and coordinate the human actions in the field of international cooperation in the peaceful uses of outer space.

18. The participants in the conference urge the great powers to sign without further delay a treaty for general and complete disarmament in order to save mankind from the scourge of war and to release energy and resources now being spent on armaments to be used for the peaceful economic and social development of all mankind. The participating countries also consider that:

(a) The non-aligned nations should be represented at all further world conferences on disarmament;

(b) All discussions on disarmament should be held under the auspices of the United Nations;

(c) General and complete disarmament should be guaranteed by an effective system of inspection and control, the teams of which should include members of non-aligned nations.

19. The participants in the conference consider it essential that an agreement on the prohibition of all nuclear and thermo-nuclear tests should be urgently concluded. With this aim in view, it is necessary that negotiations be immediately resumed, separately or as part of negotiations on general disarmament. Meanwhile, the moratorium on the testing of all nuclear weapons should be resumed and observed by all countries.

20. The participants in the conference recommend that the General Assembly of the United Nations should, at its forthcoming session, adopt a decision on the convening either of a special session of the General Assembly of the United Nations devoted to discussion of disarmament or on the convening of a world disarmament conference under the auspices of the United Nations with a view to setting in motion the process of general disarmament.

21. The participants in the conference consider that efforts should be made to remove economic imbalance inherited from colonialism and imperialism. They consider it necessary to close, through accelerated economic, industrial and agricultural development, the ever-widening gap in the standards of living between the few economically advanced countries and the many economically less-developed countries. The participants in the conference recommend the immediate establishment and operation of a United Nations capital development fund. They further agree to demand just terms of trade for the economically less-developed countries and, in particular, constructive efforts to eliminate the excessive fluctuations in primary commodity trade and the restrictive measures and practices which adversely affect the trade and revenues of the newly developing countries. In general, to demand that the fruits of the scientific and technological revolution be applied in all fields of economic development to hasten the achievement of international social justice.

22. The participating countries invite all the countries in the course of development to cooperate effectively in the

economic and commercial fields so as to face the policies of pressure in the economic sphere, as well as the harmful results which may be created by the economic blocs of the industrial countries. They invite all the countries concerned to consider to convene as soon as possible an international conference to discuss their common problems and to reach an agreement on the ways and means of repelling all damage which may hinder their development; and to discuss and agree upon the most effective measures to ensure the realization of their economic and social development.

23. The countries participating in the conference declare that the recipient countries must be free to determine the use of the economic and technical assistance which they receive, and to draw up their own plans and assign priorities in accordance with their needs.

24. The participating countries consider it essential that the General Assembly of the United Nations should, through the revision of the Charter, find a solution to the question of expanding the membership of the Security Council and of the Economic and Social Council in order to bring the composition and work of these two most important organs of the General Assembly into harmony with the needs of the organization and with the expanded membership of the United Nations.

25. The unity of the world organization and the assuring of the efficiency of its work make it absolutely necessary to evolve a more appropriate structure for the Secretariat of the United Nations, bearing in mind equitable regional distribution.

26. Those of the countries participating in the conference who recognize the Government of the People's Republic of China recommend that the General Assembly in its forthcoming session should accept the representatives of the Government of the People's Republic of China as the only legitimate representatives of that country in the United Nations.

27. The countries participating in the conference consider that the German problem is not merely a regional problem but liable to exercise a decisive influence on the course of future developments in international relations.

Concerned at the developments which have led to the present acute aggravation of the situation in regard to Germany and Berlin, the participating countries call upon all parties concerned not to resort to or threaten the use of force to solve the German question or the problem of Berlin, in accordance with the appeal made by the heads of state or government on 5th September, 1961.

The heads of state or government of non-aligned countries resolve that this declaration should be forwarded to the United Nations and brought to the attention of all the member states of the world organization. The present declaration will be also forwarded to all the other states.

The Cairo Conference

OCTOBER 5–10, 1964

OPENING ADDRESS BY
PRESIDENT GAMAL ABDEL NASSER
OF THE UNITED ARAB REPUBLIC

The people of the United Arab Republic are indeed happy to crown, with this summit conference of non-aligned countries, a year filled with great international conferences which chose this country as their seat, and so honored this land and afforded the people constant opportunities to reaffirm their faith in collective action for the sake of peace based on justice—humanity's highest ideal, hope and aspiration.

At the beginning of this year, a conference of Arab heads of state was held in Cairo.

In the middle of the year, an African summit conference convened in Cairo.

A month ago, the Arab heads of state met again in Alexandria.

Here we are now in Cairo at a conference of heads of state of non-aligned countries, adding our efforts to efforts already exerted on this land and in other peoples' countries, all endeavoring, with honor and sincerity, to consolidate the principles which, through long history, mankind has given the right of both life and death in defense and for the triumph of those principles.

It is with joy that the people of the United Arab Republic welcome you to their country, their capital, and to this very place of Cairo University where this conference is being held in a spirit of creative significance urged by the holding of an international conference on such large scale and top level, at a university which by nature holds a vanguard position in the struggle for freedom, thought, science and progress.

Our people—brothers and friends—are indeed happy that this conference should crown a year filled with conferences held on our land, and at the same time be an extension to great conferences housed by friendly peoples who gave them names of their dearest cities; of these I would mention, as an example, Bandung, Addis Ababa, Belgrade and others.

I am aware of the fact that your time is precious. Moreover, the task awaiting you in the coming few days is enormous and loaded with historical responsibilities. Therefore, I immediately request you to allow me to speak of this conference and of our joint efforts throughout. Here before you, I confess that this is a responsibility which calls for enormous effort. While I assume the responsibility of speaking of this conference, I am comforted by the fact that I shall not endeavor to go beyond a mere description of my thoughts, to place them before you and your wide experience.

In my view—brothers and friends—today we face a situation with circumstances different from those which prevailed in our September, 1961, meeting in the beautiful city of Belgrade where our dear friend President Josip Broz Tito extended to us warm hospitality.

Friends present here and who were with us in Belgrade will recall that our first conference of non-aligned countries found itself facing an issue with priority over all others at the time; by this I mean the issue of war and peace.

I trust that many of those who were with us there still have ringing in their ears that impressive call directed to us at the time by one of our sincerest friends, Jawaharlal Nehru.

At that time, in Belgrade, our friend—whose efforts are no more, but whose thoughts remain with us eternally—directed his impressive call on the issue of freedom and peace.

In that, Nehru was most successful; for the picture of the

world situation, as it appeared to us in Belgrade, was dark and fraught with danger.

The cold war at the time had reached the peak of violence and brutality.

Division of the world into two striving blocs faced us with the possibility of the cold war becoming—even by miscalculation—a definite nuclear tragedy.

Old imperialism was still waging, with ferocity, sanguinary battles, particularly in Africa.

Our anxiety for peace increased as a result of the resumption of nuclear tests in the air on the very day of our arrival in Belgrade.

It was in this shadow of danger that we met.

Since then—brothers and friends—important changes have taken place.

The cold war tension has greatly eased.

The blocs are separated although I do not say they are dissolved.

Great victories were won over imperialism. I was afforded the personal opportunity of visiting Algeria, which won her independence through the sacrifices of her valiant people. I was also afforded the opportunity of attending the ceremonies marking the evacuation from Bizerta, the aggression against which was among our preoccupations the day we met in Belgrade. I was afforded the opportunity of congratulating our dear friend President Sukarno on the restoration of a usurped portion of Indonesian territory: West Irian.

At the same time, flags of freedom were being hoisted, in the east and west of the African continent.

Then came that important and decisive step, the Moscow agreement for partial nuclear test banning, which we were delighted to sign, and to bring our wholehearted support to all subsequent steps seeking to end tension and dissipate the doubts menacing peace potentialities.

Enormous changes, no doubt. We have a right to be

happy with them and feel content that in Belgrade we wished for them, devoted our efforts to their achievement and contributed our share with all those whose eyes have opened on the grand reality of our age.

Either we all live together . . . or we all perish together. Peace in our world is indivisible.

From various parts come those who tell us that the policy of non-alignment has exhausted its role, through the changes which occurred in the international situation, particularly with regard to the cold war and the blocs policy.

We have to ask ourselves here, and in the light of the historic and human responsibility we shoulder, "Is this true?"

It is imperative for us, first, to define some of the meanings of the policy of non-alignment, thus reaffirming the declarations every one of us has made on various occasions in the past.

FIRST MEANING

The policy of non-alignment is not a trade in the strife between the two blocs, aiming at securing the highest portion of privileges from each. The proof lies in the fact that we have devoted our main efforts to the dissipation of this strife, the warning against its dangers and positive action to evade it.

SECOND MEANING

The policy of non-alignment is not passive, wishing to remain aloof of problems of its world. The proof is that we have endeavored to deal with all problems of our age and came out with solutions we set before the policy of blocs. We were bound solely by the obligation of adopting, in every situation, an attitude based on an honest view governed by no previous obligation except the principles accepted by the peoples in the most cherished document they have reached through their sacrifices, namely the Charter of the United Nations, the charter of peace based on justice.

From those two meanings, numerous facts emerge:

1) The policy of non-alignment is not a cold war trade.

2) The changes in the situation of world blocs have no bearing on the policy of non-alignment.

This policy retains its expression of humanity's conscience bound by the United Nations Charter, irrespective of the existence of two, three or four blocs.

3) In its final form, the attitude of non-alignment is a policy for the sake of peace based on justice.

Having reached that point, it is only natural that we should ask ourselves:

"Has our demand and objective, 'Peace based on Justice,' been realized?"

If this has been achieved, then our work here has reached its happy ending. We should just have to restrict our efforts to the safeguarding of what we have accomplished there at the United Nations headquarters alone.

Yet, we regret that this has not been achieved, although our dearest wish remains the accomplishment of this aim.

Our most cherished wish is for the day when there will be no groupings outside the United Nations headquarters. Then will humanity be close to its lofty ideal.

This—as I have mentioned, brothers and friends—is still to be achieved.

I ask myself, what then, has been accomplished? What is the significance of those enormous changes which, we all agree, have taken place, and with which we have welcomed and congratulated those who worked for their achievement, ourselves included?

We have to admit that we have covered part of the route; but, what stage is it exactly that we have achieved?

A sound assessment of the latent meanings behind the new changes, without resorting to exaggerated pessimism or optimism, underlines that the most outstanding achievement is the fact that the spectacular scientific progress, particularly in the sphere of the power of nuclear destruction and the means of carrying it with long-range missiles, has opened many eyes to the reality which all peoples of the world, ours included, and all peace aspirations including our own, called for, namely, that it is impossible for humanity to face an eventual nuclear war.

Spectacular scientific progress, which would at the same time be terrifying if it should get out of hand, has reached —though indirectly—the stage where it could support and strengthen the argument of those who staunchly adhered to the necessity of keeping clear from the brink of the abyss.

All have come to realize clearly that mankind has no third choice.

Either all men live together in peace, or the entire human race would commit suicide, and destroy itself by itself.

This scientific progress which is at once spectacular and terrifying, has recorded the impossibility of war.

Yet, the question we—once again—have to insist on answering is: Does the impossibility of war automatically mean the establishment of peace?

We all admit that great and serious differences exist between the two issues.

War has become impossible . . . yet, peace also is still remote.

Stress on the impossibility of war was among the arguments we pressed in our call for peace.

Stress on the impossibility of war was among the supporters of the logic with which we submitted our case to world public opinion.

Yet, the mere reaching of a position where all should discover the impossibility of war was not our ultimate aim.

Our final objective is peace based on justice. This, we still have to achieve; and, as a result, our aim remains before us, awaiting all the efforts we can deploy.

We would even go beyond that in our statement.

We would declare that the world could one morning

find itself, once again, on the brink of nuclear war, if one of the powers succeeded in achieving a scientific and military advantage with a clear bearing on the balance of power which imposes the present truce.

Surprise events can also occur at any time and any place in the world, which would make any of the great world powers imagine—even through pride—that its vital and delicate interests are exposed to a danger which it cannot remove, except by involving itself. Repercussions lacking enough and sound control to bear on this power.

Here, we find that the position of the present truce is promising.

Yet, at the same time, we find that this situation calls for our endeavors, rather additional efforts on ours and on the part of others, so that the unstable truce might develop into a world peace, or else a boundless setback would surprise us, when least expected.

From here comes our assessment of the role and action of this conference. Its role is to study the means by which it can bear the enormous changes brought upon the international situation—and which imposed that truce based on nuclear balance and nuclear terror combined—to genuine peace.

As for the action, it is to trace from here a road to peace, or at least to contribute with our thoughts and collective efforts to the discovery of that only path to salvation.

This is the great challenge facing us.

How can the truce of balance and terror be transformed into lasting peace?

Then, where is the road to genuine and lasting peace?

If I may be allowed to pursue this attempt at reviewing the matter with you, it is my opinion and the view of the United Arab Republic delegation that the landmarks we see on the road to peace appear to us as follows:

First: Imperialism in all its forms and kinds, old and new, the overt and the secret, must vanish.

Imperialism as we understand it—considering that it is the domination of one country by another and its exploitation with the terror of force or through treaties and prerogatives which can survive only by the terror of force—has become humiliating to our age, and is the cause of dangerous explosions which cannot be stopped and their impact cannot be reduced through any artificial operation which does not pull out the roots of evil.

Under the imperialist heading we place a number of branches.

We place the policies of armed suppression, as we can see in the Portuguese colonies, in the occupied Arab south, in Aden and in Oman.

We place the policies of military pacts and bases, as we can observe in most continents of the world.

We place the policies of seizing the land of peoples and ousting them by force and with the support of imperialism, as in the case of Palestine. We place the policies of racial discrimination and segregation, as we can see in South Africa.

The most advanced means of hiding and concealment is no longer able to force the peoples to be content under foreign domination, be it political, military, economic or cultural.

Second: The painful disparity in the living standards of peoples will only serve to place the world on the brink of a volcano that will never calm down or rest.

There is a terrifying disparity between the advanced states and the underdeveloped countries. What adds to the feeling of those differences is the fact that the peoples of underdeveloped countries find—and rightly too—that the prosperity of others was wrenched from them through shocking imperialist looting.

We here in the United Arab Republic and many, if not

most, of you face the tragedy we lived for centuries, during which our saved national wealth was removed and drained with systematic brutality.

While we place our feelings and aspirations above any grudge, we find that the simplest rules of justice make it imperative that those seeking progress should meet with genuine cooperation on the part of those who preceded them to such advancement.

Today, the demand for social justice is the driving force of events in more than one country. This demand—the demand for justice, is about to perform the same role in the community of nations, in a world which, despite its size is becoming one entity, where distance counts no more, thanks to revolutionary progress in means of communications.

We do not want world partitioning to end up with a Western and an Eastern bloc so that new, bigger and more serious divisions might follow:

A bloc of the poor and a bloc of the wealthy.

A bloc of the advanced and a bloc of the underdeveloped.

A bloc in the north of our universe with rights to prosperity and a bloc in the south with nothing but deprivation.

A bloc of whites and a bloc of colored.

Poverty and wealth cannot live in peace side by side. Progress and underdevelopment cannot live in peace side by side. Prosperity and deprivation cannot live in peace side by side.

We live in one world. . . . We form one human race, no matter how different colors may be. Here, we submit the following points:

1. It is high time a revision was made of the contracts of old prerogatives which hand over the wealth of many countries to other states at no fair price.

2. It is high time we insisted on raising the price of raw materials we or most of us give so that it might be compatible with the price of manufactured goods which we or most of

us try to obtain in implementation of our aspirations to development. We have tried to coordinate our efforts in the development and trade conferences in Cairo and Geneva, but the road before us is long and difficult.

3. It is high time those who preceded along the route of advancement realized that their cooperation with those trying to reach that advancement means neither despotic conditions nor giving alms.

This is not necessary for us alone, it is essential to others as well, because it is vital to peace.

Third: Standing in the way of the historic, political, economic, social and cultural development of the peoples aspiring to freedom is an action by the great powers which must be stopped.

We should afford the peoples the opportunity of reshaping their lives anew even through trial and error, considering that this is the only and sure path to progress.

We see dangerous features around us, developing with no treatment. Small wars are breaking out in more than one place in Asia, Africa and Latin America.

Internal coups directed and engineered by the secret organs of the big powers are being repeated before us every day.

Attempts at infiltration by imperialist means are being paved by leaps and bounds; they even find formations taking the shape of countries and which in fact are a mere mask and veil. The trade of foreign mercenaries is now practiced without honor or shame, and under circumstances which could lead to serious consequences.

Open attempts at psychological impressions on peoples fill parts of all the world continents, spreading the seeds of instability in every land.

Fourth: The United Nations Charter should absorb the new facts forged by an experience of twenty years since its declaration, particularly that the period was revolutionary and eventful; this great organization should develop to the standard of the aspirations which formed it. All must cease deteriorating it and transforming it into a mere tool in the service of the policy of the strong.

The United Nations must accept the aspirations of all peoples looking forward to freedom and progress.

The United Nations must have room for all peoples. A people like that of China—numbering one-third of the world's population—should not be deprived of its legitimate seat at the United Nations.

The United Nations must have room for justice with peace; peace cannot survive without justice. Belief that justice can be overlooked by resorting to the *fait accompli,* even if it should be based on injustice, is a dangerous hallucination which not only shakes the meaning of justice alone, but shakes with it the meaning of peace.

While I state this, as a further indication to the cause of the Palestine people, I am not thrusting upon you a problem related to our region alone, but rather, I speak of a problem which concerns the entire world, as long as it is concerned with the problem of peace anywhere.

What happened in Palestine is dangerous, and in its danger, is equal to, if not more dangerous, than what happens before us today in Southern Rhodesia. Concealed behind and in connivance with the Zionist movement, imperialism usurped part of the very heart of the Arab nation, ousted its people and established in the center of the Arab land an armed hostile base menacing the aspiration to Arab freedom, the aspiration to Arab unity and the aspiration to Arab progress.

Fifth: Total and complete disarmament can, after all that, be achieved following steps which made it possible and paved the way for it.

One of the outstanding accomplishments resulting from the Belgrade conference was the fact that the non-aligned countries were party to the disarmament talks and increased their knowledge of the dimensions of the problem, and so increased the ability to contribute to a solution.

Disarmament has long remained the hope of mankind which suffered from the horrors and tragedies of warfare.

Yet, the development of armament today does not make of it mere wars and tragedies but makes of it a gate to destruction in a manner never before conceived by the human mind. Moreover, the fantastic budgets needed for modern armaments can be the main force leading to development plans.

The great Bandung conference marked the stand of many free peoples against the evils of imperialism.

The great Belgrade conference marked the stand of many free peoples against the perils of war.

This conference in Cairo, pursuing the extended struggle which is getting deeper and bigger day after day, is worthy of being the conference for the consolidation of peace through international cooperation.

The impressive assembly in this hall of peoples' leaders, and liberation movement heroes, together with the principles every one of them represents and the common objectives which made possible their meeting today and which are demanded as a vital necessity of our age—that all renders this place more suitable than any other for the proclamation of the principles of international cooperation and international behavior, tracing the route of action for peace based on justice.

If, in a final summing up, we should be allowed to define some of the thoughts which should be given priority in that declaration, we propose that stress be laid on the following principles:

1. Peace is not the mere avoidance of the use of force; it is also, as Article 55 of the United Nations Charter stipulates, "The creation of conditions of stability and well-being

which are necessary for peaceful and friendly relations among nations based on respect for the principle of equal rights and self-determination of people."

2. Realization of the conditions and circumstances vital to peace is a matter concerning all countries; the issue is given weight by the fact that they all share in the responsibility.

3. Endeavor to avoid the use of force in international relations cannot be successful by the mere adherence to finding a solution to every problem separately and in isolation of others, but what would bring success to such endeavor would be the existence of a sound understanding of peace based on justice.

Justice alone leads to lasting peace; force might, for some time, succeed in imposing itself on a certain situation, but, even with the *fait accompli* it builds up, it remains far from the meaning and maintenance of peace.

4. Peace cannot be stable if it relies on the stagnation of unjust situations; for countries to respect their treaty obligations means the honoring of genuine treaties freely concluded and which are not in contradiction with the United Nations Charter; thus, the obligation of countries to honor their treaties must be compatible with Article 103 of the Charter which stipulates that "In the event of a conflict between the obligations of the members of the United Nations under the present Charter and their obligations under any other international agreement, their obligations under the present Charter shall prevail."

5. Cooperation among countries and understanding among peoples cannot be achieved in an effective and definite manner unless the differences in the living standards of the various peoples are removed and their equal rights are confirmed to them all.

Since we are aware that progress endeavors are first and foremost the responsibility of those who seek that progress and their constant efforts to achieve it, it is their right that no obstacles be set on their way through pressure or maneuvers; all must realize, on the other hand, that in its essence peace is an association of prosperity covering the entire universe.

I found fit to review before you, in a general way, a picture of our thought, as we are about to begin this great conference and define the aims of its action.

May God Almighty support your aspirations and endeavors, and may the torches of guidance rise on your way—the way to peace.

ADDRESS BY
PRESIDENT JOSIP BROZ TITO
OF YUGOSLAVIA

I am very happy to have the honor, on behalf of the peoples of Yugoslavia and in my own name, of greeting this eminent gathering which, I am fully confident, will contribute to the achievement of the lofty ideals to which the peoples of all countries aspire.

May I, first of all, express my heartfelt gratitude to our dear friend President Gamal Abdel Nasser and to the people of the United Arab Republic for their truly friendly reception. I would also like to pay tribute to the government of the United Arab Republic for their highly successful organization of the conference. It is particularly gratifying to me that we are meeting in Cairo and that this gathering is being held on the soil of Africa, a continent which is the symbol of the dynamic changes in the present-day world, and of the striving for a life of freedom and equality in the international community.

May I also express our appreciation to the participants in the preparatory meeting in Colombo and in the standing committee of ambassadors, and to the foreign ministers who spared no efforts to help make this a successful conference.

Looking back upon our earlier gathering in Belgrade, I can but call to mind with a feeling of grief and deep respect the memory of a distinguished champion of the policy of peace and non-alignment and great leader of the Indian people, Jawaharlal Nehru, who worked so untiringly for the fulfillment of the ideals which have led us also to meet here today.

I am certain that we all regard with gratification this large gathering of the most responsible statesmen. The similarity of our views, our common strivings and determination to contribute to the strengthening of the policy of peace and to the establishment of better and more equitable relations in the world have brought us together here.

My country had the great honor of being host to the First Conference of Heads of State or Government of Non-Aligned Countries, which made an important contribution to the improvement of the international situation.

A far larger number of countries has now gathered at this conference in Cairo. This attests the growing affirmation of the policy pursued by the non-aligned countries and reflects the significant changes and new conditions that have emerged in the world, the increased power and influence of the policy of peace and of active peaceful co-existence. The attainment of independence by a large number of countries in Africa, associated in the Organization of African Unity, and their active participation in international affairs, is of tremendous importance for the goals towards which we aspire. The large participation of these countries in the present conference lends special strength to our action. I note with satisfaction that Angola, which is fighting for its independence, is an active participant in the conference.

I should like to welcome the presence at this conference of a considerable number of Latin American countries, Finland, the representatives of numerous liberation movements and other organizations. This is an indication of how close our policy is also to the movements fighting for independence and which find a strong support in this conference. It is my profound conviction that all this is of far-reaching significance and indicates that the interests of peace cannot be separated from those of freedom and progress, and are common to all nations.

Reviewing the events which have taken place since our first conference, we are further strengthened in our conviction of the vitality of the policy which strives for equitable relations among states and nations and confirmed in our belief that the growth of its influence was inevitable. It has become apparent that this policy is neither inhibited by geographical limits nor tainted with racial prejudices, nor hampered by differences in social systems, but that it is rather, by drawing strength from the progressive changes that have occurred, acquiring a growing measure of support. Our commitment to the principles of peace and to new, more equitable relations in the world has not lost its significance as a consequence of the easing of tensions; on the contrary these developments have opened fresh possibilities and indicated the need for further activity.

At the time of the Belgrade conference, and after it as well, the attempt to form a "third bloc" was frequently imputed to those championing the policy of co-existence. This showed a lack of understanding of the substance of this policy, and reflected the spirit of the cold war and a failure to grasp contemporary trends. If there is any objection that might be raised in regard to the role of the non-aligned countries, then it could only be that they have occasionally failed to react with sufficient speed and unity to certain negative developments. Today the reproaches regarding a "third force" are hardly heard any longer. In actual fact, the military-political groupings have lost much of their rigor, and their function and their place in international affairs have changed somewhat, as have relationships within them. The policy of peaceful settlement of controversial problems, of the easing of international tension, of acceleration of economic development and of de-colonization, rallies within the United Nations and at other major international gatherings a growing number of countries and forces—some of them not represented here—which are desirous of contributing to the stabilization of conditions in the world on new, sounder foundations. This policy is no longer so much characterized by formal non-alignment, or alignment, which we know may be relative concepts—as such formulas are becoming increasingly outdated—but above all is reflected in active and principled endeavor, in a unity of action in the application of the principles of the policy of active and peaceful co-existence. This policy introduces new dimensions into contemporary political developments in the world, for it makes broad cooperation possible not on the basis of any sort of artificial or formal alignment, but rather in accordance with a unity of interest, and in the light of independent assessments.

I believe we share a common conviction that the situation today is somewhat better than it was at the time of the Belgrade conference, that the development of international relations during that period was basically positive and that our first gathering gauged correctly the general interest and the trends of international events. Although doubts were expressed at that time in various quarters and resistance even offered to the ideas and proposals of the conference, subsequent developments have confirmed the correctness of our appraisals and also our conviction—shared today by all reasonable persons and by responsible statesmen—that in this nuclear era the basic problems of the world must be settled by peaceful means.

Looking back upon the period that has elapsed, we may note with gratification that our countries, primarily within the United Nations but also outside that organization, have together with all other peace-loving countries and forces, helped make the voice of reason heard and respected, especially during fateful moments of crisis in international relations. Although they did not have strong military and economic potentials at their disposal, our countries have—

through their moral and political standing—succeeded in winning growing respect for their positions.

Undoubtedly, the most striking example of this activity was the United Nations Conference on Trade and Development, the initiative for which originated at the Belgrade conference. Similarly useful is the role the non-aligned countries are playing and the efforts they are investing in the disarmament talks conducted by the eighteen-nation committee in Geneva.

The non-aligned countries, in association with other peace-loving and progressive forces, have contributed a great deal to accelerating the process of de-colonization. We need but recall that the Belgrade conference extended significant support to the liberation struggle of the Algerian people.

As the non-aligned countries have maintained, it has been proved that negotiations can gradually decrease differences in opposing points of view and enlarge the area of understanding. Although agreements which would eliminate the root of the danger of nuclear war have not yet been reached and, although the arms race unfortunately still persists, nevertheless, after a lengthy cold war period, the world witnessed the first well-known direct agreements between the leading nuclear powers. I have in mind here, in the first place, the Moscow treaty on the partial banning of nuclear tests. This agreement and other measures caused a feeling of relief and met with the resolute support of the large majority of states and of world public opinion.

In line with this, I think we may conclude that there has also been a slackening of tension over the German question, a settlement of which should be sought primarily through negotiations between the two German states, thereby enabling the German people to decide on their future.

As tension relaxes, better prospects are opening up for the peoples fighting against colonialism and imperialism, notwithstanding the fact that many difficulties still stand in the way and that old, obsolete conceptions and practices have not yet been overcome.

In contrast to the times when a relatively small number of countries took part in international life and when the main role belonged to only a restricted circle of powers, we now find a number of newly independent states on the world scene. It is therefore no longer possible in international cooperation to neglect the interests of individual states, and even less of entire regions, for no nation will now accept to remain in a subordinate position.

Never before in the world have there been so many diverse forms of development, nor at the same time such a degree of interdependence. Every crisis and every injustice done to a nation has repercussions in all directions, but so has every success achieved. Is it not an absurdity that even today, when any foolhardy military adventure can bring about a general nuclear catastrophe, we are still faced with military interventions and threats of force?

In the altered picture of the world, positive processes in one way or another involve many countries which have begun to discard the criteria of predetermined attitudes dating back to the times of the cold war. The vital national interests of many peoples, until recently thwarted, thereby find growing expression. These interests will continue to require the promotion of a policy of peace and international cooperation on a footing of equality, within which they can alone find adequate realization. One-sided solutions, which rely on force and narrowly conceived ideological motives, are gradually giving way to, and must be replaced by, new forms of association among free peoples and sovereign states, predicated on recognition of their national interests. That is why development on the basis of national independence, the equal rights of peoples and the struggle for peace, are indivisible. The aim of our efforts should, in my opinion, be to encourage and facilitate this process, and I feel that therein lies the essence of our policy and of our political action. The relationship of forces has already undergone a fundamental change in this sense and is further changing in favor of peace and of universal progress.

One of the primary conditions for the consolidation of peace and the establishment of equal and more humane relations in the world continues to be the accelerated and final liquidation of colonialism. It would appear that only a few strongholds of colonialism remain but these, although they often cover a relatively small territory and population, seriously jeopardize the stabilization of broader areas and constitute a source of neo-colonialist and other dangers to newly independent countries. It is evident that resolute efforts must be made both within the United Nations and outside the organization in order to ensure early and full independence to all peoples who are still under colonial domination. I am referring, primarily, to the people of Angola, Southern Rhodesia, Mozambique, of the so-called Portuguese Guinea, of Aden, South-West Africa, British Guiana and others. Similarly, racial discrimination and its most odious form—apartheid—in the Republic of South Africa, are a disgrace to mankind today. We must strive to have the sanctions against the Government of the Republic of South Africa, demanded by the United Nations and the Organization of African Unity, put into effect. It is also necessary resolutely to oppose all other attempts at dividing peoples along racial lines.

We all agree that it is necessary to remove the inequalities which exist at present in the world economy. Accelerating the development of the less developed countries is one of the most vital problems of the contemporary world and should therefore become the concern of the entire international community. Naturally, it is up to the peoples in developing countries to activate their potential economic forces in the efforts to achieve economic progress and equality.

Obviously, we do not wish to deprive ourselves of any opportunity for economic cooperation on an equal footing that accelerates the development of our countries. There is hardly any need to stress here that assistance to the developing countries is an obligation and that it is also in the interest of the developed countries. Such assistance is therefore of mutual benefit and for this reason should be granted with respect for the independence and equality of nations and their national development plans. Regrettably, tendencies to retard the economic emancipation of developing countries, and thus to subjugate them, still exist. This new aspect of imperialism and neo-colonialism constitutes a grave threat and could, if not resolutely resisted, jeopardize what has already been achieved.

The relaxation of tension will make it possible to bring the attention of world public opinion, with greater ease, to the existing international economic problems. This was clearly confirmed by the United Nations Conference on Trade and Development, where, more than ever before, it was demonstrated that the world today is interdependent in economic terms as well, and that the problems of accelerated economic development can be most successfully coped with by establishing universal economic relations, devoid of discrimination and ideological prejudices. This would pave the way for more profound structural changes and a new international division of labor.

One of the more significant characteristics of the conference lies in that, by constituting itself into a permanent organ of the U.N., it has afforded the possibility for the future solution of those questions which could not be solved at this time. The unity which the developing countries forged at the Geneva conference on the basis of their common interests was not made use of for the purpose of imposing fictitious decisions or of having decisions adopted by declaratory votes; on the contrary, generally acceptable solutions were sought. This unity should be further developed through new endeavors to advance the work so well begun. I am certain that implementation of the positive conclusions of the Geneva conference, which we resolutely support, and participation in the preparations for, and work of, similar gatherings will constitute one of the most significant components of our activity in the future as well.

The further improvement of international relations and the settlement of basic controversial problems in the world depends, in essence, upon the progress made in the field of disarmament which has been and continues to be the key issue. We are all aware how much disarmament could contribute to more rapid economic development. The contention still heard from certain individuals in some of the developed countries to the effect that disarmament would cause great economic and social difficulties is absurd. To accept such a thesis would be tantamount to asserting that there is no more room in these countries and the world at large, for peacetime, socially useful production. Naturally this is nonsense, if we bear in mind the present advancement of science and technology, and in line with it the rapid growth of human requirements.

The declaration of our first conference already stressed the need for general and complete disarmament. It is essential, in my opinion, that the present conference should also resolutely demand that a beginning be made at long last in solving the question of general disarmament. I believe that I share the views of all those present at this gathering when I state that we expect more determined moves in this respect, especially from the great powers. On their part, the countries participating in this conference should in future condemn even more boldly and with a greater measure of solidarity all negative developments in international relations which may serve certain countries as a pretext for continuing the arms race.

We have always supported partial measures as well, designed gradually to lead to general and complete disarmament. There is no doubt that, given good will on both sides, agreements could be reached on the banning of underground nuclear tests, on prohibiting the dissemination of nuclear weapons, on setting up atom-bomb-free zones in various regions of the world, as well as on the elimination of bases and the withdrawal of troops from foreign territories, their military importance having in any case decreased considerably.

For all these reasons it would be necessary—either in the General Assembly of the United Nations, at a special session, or at a special disarmament conference—to consider all these problems and adopt decisions required by the security of mankind. Perhaps the General Assembly or a special conference, depending upon an appraisal of the degree of realism of certain measures, could recommend the convening of special conferences for the purpose of achieving specific agreements. In this way, and through the inclusion of other states, the number of participants in negotiations would be increased, which is fully justified because disarmament directly affects the entire international community.

I am certain that this conference will, like the one held in Belgrade, give strong support to the United Nations and to all the positive achievements and prospects it offers to mankind today, for the United Nations whose bodies should be enlarged in tone with the change in the number and composition of its members constitutes an indispensable factor of peace and international cooperation. We feel that the United Nations should in future display an even greater measure of initiative with regard to all those questions relating to the strengthening of peace in the world. Of course, the attainment of universality by the United Nations is of major importance and continues to be our common task.

The codification of the principles of peaceful and active co-existence by the United Nations—to which I also referred at the fifteenth session of the General Assembly of the United Nations—should contribute precisely to strengthening the role of the world organization. Adoption of the principles of co-existence as norms governing the life of the international community would enrich the United Nations Charter both in substance and with respect to its practical application. I therefore feel that our conference should consider the question of codification of the principles of active and peaceful co-existence, adopt relevant conclusions and submit proposals along these lines to the United Nations.

Regrettably, events have occurred of late which jeopardize the relaxation of tension that has already been achieved and give cause for concern. In Southeast Asia, Cyprus, in the Congo, around Cuba, and elsewhere, there are still displays of the policy of force and of gross interference in the domestic affairs of the countries concerned. Even military intervention, which can in no way be justified, is resorted to.

It is with anxiety that we witness developments in Southeast Asia. In South Vietnam brutal foreign interference constantly threatens to expand the conflict to neighboring countries. Serious concern is also caused by the recent so-called reprisals against the Democratic Republic of Vietnam. Existing agreements have for some time been openly violated in Laos. Pressure from the outside is also being brought to bear on Cambodia and its territorial integrity is not respected. Yugoslavia considers that the proposal advanced by Prince Sihanouk on guarantees for the neutrality of Cambodia deserves attention and support, as do other proposals to put an end to outside interference in this part of the world.

The Cyprus crisis is also largely the result of a policy of pressure and interference from outside, which renders more difficult the settlement of internal conditions in the interest of both ethnical groups. Naturally, it is necessary above all to take into account the interests and desire of the people of Cyprus and their government.

We are also witnessing a succession of various forms of interference in the Congo, which has been going on ever since the proclamation of its independence, obstructing the badly needed stabilization and the unimpeded development of this country within the community of independent African states.

We are aware of the fact that there are many unsettled border problems in the world. We feel that in the still complex present-day situation, they should not be raised in a way that might lead to conflict. On the contrary, their solution should be sought in a peaceful manner, by way of negotiations between the countries directly concerned.

At this point, I should like to direct your attention to some harmful notions which are used to justify the policy of intervention. According to them it is possible to accept peace and co-existence in one area, while defending one's interest with force and pressure in other, supposedly marginal areas or in relations with small countries, by invoking ideological or other motives and supporting cold war methods. The assumption here apparently being that the other side will not dare to react for the sake of peace and that peoples exposed to this will be forced to accept such a policy. In fact these circles wish deliberately to distort the meaning of co-existence by interpreting it as signifying the maintenance of the political status quo in areas where vestiges of colonialism and dependence still exist. Or else they erroneously explain co-existence as implying a halt in social development.

There is another no less harmful concept, based on the same premise, which seeks to place the policy of co-existence in opposition to the liberation struggle of peoples, and therefore advocates the need and the usefulness of a renewed aggravation of international relations, not even precluding the possibility of a general conflagration. It is obvious that there can be no peace without freedom, but under the present conditions it is also true that there can be no freedom without peace.

Such theories are, each in its own way, untenable and foster one another, impeding unity of action on the part of the growing forces of peace.

The source of crisis lies in the resistance which reactionary and hegemonistic forces are offering to the policy of co-existence, that is, in the overt violation of its fundamental principles, and more particularly of the principles of sovereignty and self-determination. For this reason I feel that our conference should resolutely request all states consistently to apply the principles of active and peaceful co-existence in all regions of the world and in international relations in their entirety.

The experiences which history has handed down to us show that aggressors tend to interpret any hesitation on the part of the threatened nations, and on that of all peace-loving forces, as a weakness and are thereby still further encouraged. Under the present conditions, it is more than ever necessary to concert our efforts and to give permanence to our actions. Our cooperation in the United Nations has made quite good progress and yielded considerably fruitful results. Mutual consultations and joint actions within the United Nations should become part of a regular practice, as should also co-operation with all other countries desiring peace.

May I turn once again to the policy of non-alignment, the basic tenet of which is the preservation of peace and active and peaceful co-existence among peoples and states.

This policy arose, among other things, from the need of many countries, particularly of the newly liberated countries, to resist the tendencies towards creating divisions between states in the period of the cold war, and to safeguard and strengthen their independence, thus, at the same time securing the necessary conditions for their unhampered economic and social development. Since its inception, it has worked towards rallying peace-loving countries and movements and towards encouraging progressive trends. This being its substance, the policy of non-alignment never was, nor could ever be, a policy of passive resistance to the division of the world, or a policy of equidistance. It was always principled and universal in its approach, committed when the preservation of peace and the protection of the fundamental rights of peoples and states were involved. For that reason, it was only natural that our policy should have contributed to the overcoming of the cold war and the division of the world and, in line with general development, should have become one of the decisive factors of the general movement for peace and progress, as it reflects objective and long-range interests— both national and general.

Our policy is related, in the most practical sense, to the requirements of peoples and states. This makes it possible for us to propose solutions which are practicable in existing circumstances. For this reason, the policy of the countries struggling for new international relations has grown into a realistic progressive platform regarding the development of the international community. As for our mutual relations, they should be particularly imbued by a spirit of friendship, understanding, conciliation and readiness to solve all existing problems either by bilateral or, if necessary, multilateral contacts, because our mutual solidarity is of significance for all our future activities and successes.

None of us at this gathering claims to have a monopoly over peace-loving initiatives or the policy of peace. It is obvious that great responsibility for exploring the avenues leading to a further relaxation of tension and to agreements lies with the leading nuclear powers. However, negotiations and agreements among the leading nuclear powers can be successful only if they enjoy the support of the international community. It is certain that this support shall not be lacking if account is taken of the interests of all countries, big and small alike, and if their rights and equality are respected. Otherwise, such negotiations and agreements can hardly be what they are meant to be—factors of stabilization and peace in the world as a whole. As far as we are concerned, we shall, of course, resolutely support all constructive initiatives and agreements that are reached in this spirit.

It is my firm belief that if we wish to save the world from catastrophe, to secure social progress and a happier future for all nations and people, we must and, indeed, can solve the existing problems only within the general efforts to ensure peace and international cooperation on a basis of equality, that is, in line with the principles of active peaceful co-existence. The attainment of these goals calls for the activity and unity of all peace-loving countries.

EXCERPT FROM ADDRESS BY PRESIDENT AHMED SUKARNO OF INDONESIA

. . . Another change of significance for us since 1961 lies in the field of international peace and security. Today the problem of security is no longer a problem directly related to the big powers. They can take care of themselves. It is a matter of fact that, during these last few years, they have reached a condition of some balance. In the political, military and economic fields they cannot destroy one another. They are equally strong and will not wage war against one another since war to them means total annihilation in which they would lose everything. They will co-exist with one another, they will even co-exist in peace with one another, because they have no alternative to that course. The risk of losing all they have is too great.

But the problem of security is still grave. However, it now resides in security connected with the struggles for independence and in the security of the developing nations once independence has been won.

Because all else is useless when our security is under serious threat, this is the most important matter for our attention, with all other political and economic items of our agenda subservient to it. The security of the developing countries is a prerequisite for their development.

Since the Belgrade conference, it cannot be said that our security has been improved. I would even say there has been deterioration in the situation for the developing countries. Just look at the situation everywhere in the world! Southeast Asia is a turbulent sea of insecurity, with outside, imperialist forces disturbing the security of Vietnam, Laos, Cambodia, and the so-called "Federation of Malaysia" and surrounding areas. Then there is the Middle East. There is Cyprus, there is the Congo and the problems of the African continent in general, and there is Yemen, Aden and there is Cuba as an example of insecurity in Latin America. And these are but a few of the cases where the developing countries are afflicted with persistent insecurity. Because this insecurity is merely the symptom caused by the old forces trying might and main to preserve their interests in the face of our efforts to build our societies in line with the new norms of the rising order of a new world, it is quite inevitable that this insecurity will continue, and will even increase. I do not see any speedy end to this situation. On the contrary I believe that more cases will soon arise.

If we are not aware of the new tactics being used by the forces of the old order, if we are not alert to their machinations, above all, if we lose our sense of solidarity, we can be sure that old powers will rush in, like air into a vacuum, to secure, to maintain or to restore their interests and their old established order.

If I am not greatly mistaken in my reading of the situation, the problem of world peace itself now resides in the question of the security of the developing nations. Persistent insecurity in these new states can spark off the fire of local domestic conflict. This can spread at the edges like a flame in the grass and develop into conflict with neighbors; and then into conflict throughout a region. Is this not precisely what we can see happening before our very eyes today? I know I do not need to give examples! And once a conflict has spread region-wide, it constitutes—if not before—a standing invitation to involvement of the big power blocs. Yes! World peace today is a problem of how to achieve security for the developing nations during this period of transition to a new order in the world.

There is another important item of our agenda where I am convinced we must look behind the obvious on the surface to the underlying forces of domination beneath. That is the matter of peaceful co-existence.

As compared with our common understanding of the reason for the struggle for national liberation from colonialism and imperialism, our understanding of peaceful co-existence cannot, perhaps, be entirely taken for granted.

Certainly, much has already been said and written about it, and surely we are in general well agreed. However, it is a new term, and when we search below the surface, it is possible that unwittingly we are not talking about quite the same thing. It is true that this has now won wide acceptance. It is in common use among the capitalist group, among the communist group. It is in common use among the countries of Asia, Africa and Latin America, as well as, of course, among ourselves, the participants in the non-aligned countries' conference. If however, in spite of its common usage, we interpret its underlying principles in different ways, it is possible that among us of the nonaligned countries we will interpret peaceful co-existence in different ways in practice, and this might even influence our foreign outlook as well as changing our course of action.

Originally, as you know, peaceful co-existence was a term related to the war of ideologies, that is the war between the capitalist and the communist ideologies. Even for the agenda of our first non-aligned countries' conference we spoke of— and I quote—"peaceful co-existence among states with different political and social systems."

Well, sisters and brothers, you probably know what I think about ideological wars! Already in Belgrade I remarked that "ideological conflict need not lead to tension. It must not lead to tension." Oh, no! In our age, ideologies will not create a big power conflict leading to a world conflagration. What endangers world peace is the conflict of national interests in the international field, both bilaterally and multilaterally. These are the sources from which a world conflagration might spring. The ideological conflict is merely a disguise to involve the innocent on one side or the other, as the imperialist powers search for or try to preserve their domination over the world.

And see what came to pass after the crisis over Berlin at the time of our first conference in Belgrade! From that conference we expressed our great concern, from that conference we sent envoys to Moscow and to Washington. Today it is becoming obvious that, with regard to the ideological conflict, great progress has been made between the two power blocs—I hope that it began because of our intervention from Belgrade. At least it is certain that the protagonists of the conflicting ideologies have discovered ample reasons to live side by side, without trying to wipe each other off the face of the earth. They are reaching an accommodation if only because they feel mutually protected by their huge arsenals of nuclear deterrents.

Certainly, this item of our agenda needs our full attention, but, I submit, in another direction. I think we can have full confidence in the ability of Moscow and Washington to find additional accommodation and increased rapprochement. I am convinced that they will continue to co-exist peacefully, and with increasing ease. I think we should compliment them on their achievement. Long live peaceful co-existence between Moscow and Washington! I do not think they are in need of us at this present juncture!

However, we will do well to transfer our attention and to exert our energies upon a more complicated and more urgent matter.

And that is the serious problem of peaceful co-existence between the old forces of domination and the new developing nations. Allow me to throw out some questions to show you in what direction my thoughts turn.

How can any nation co-exist in peace when surrounding military bases and economic strongholds are used to subvert or to manipulate its domestic activities? How can a nation peacefully co-exist with an outside power that dominates its policies? How can a nation live side by side in peace with states which prevent it from establishing the social and economic systems suited to its national identity?

Look at the military bases scattered all over the world! Look at the military bases of the big powers built in all strategic positions—look at them still being built today! Those foreign bases, sisters and brothers, are said to be for the purpose of containing alien ideologies. But that is nonsense! See how they are used today. They are used against the newly developing countries. They are used to preserve the interests of the old imperialist order. They are used as the paramount vehicle of imperialist interests in the newly developing countries.

But military bases are not the only instruments used by the forces of imperialism to preserve their old order of domination of the world. Oh, no!

Is it a matter of racial discrimination or apartheid?— What is this but a question of domination of race by race or of nation by nation for the sake of preserving the interests of the dominator? Is it a matter of economic subservience? What is this but a question of domination of nation by nation for the sake of preserving, of strengthening, of promoting and extending the interests of the dominator? Is it a matter of the founding of new states that are independent in name but not in substance—not in factual practice? What is it but a question of the domination of nation by nation for the sake of preserving or expanding the interests of the dominator?

Here in this matter of domination lies the source of our weakness. Here in this matter of the persistent determination of the forces of the old order to maintain their privileges, their interests, their power in the world, lies the source of our division. This is the question upon which we must concentrate our attention. This is the question upon the solution of which we must concentrate our energies.

I know, sisters and brothers, that we need development, especially do we need economic development. I am well aware that we need greater technical skills, that we need to build industries, that we need more material goods for our people, who still suffer want and shortages of all kinds.

But we MUST understand—we MUST, we MUST—that it will not work just to turn our attention to economic development and social welfare and to ignore the diversion of our efforts to serve the interests of the old powers. How can it work? How can it work if the very basis of our economic structure diverts the products of our soil to the coffers of the giant corporations of the capitalist world? How can it work if the method of our economic endeavor diverts the proceeds of our toil to the pockets of the same old foreign-based institutions which exploited us in our colonial days?

We MUST understand that economic development will bring benefits to our people only when we have torn up by their roots all the institutions, all the links that make us subservient in any way, in any fashion, to the old order of domination.

Our problems of economic development are not unsurmountable if only we are left to our own devices, if only domination does not creep in to divert our activities, to subvert our endeavors, to bring deviation from our purposes, to cause division among us. It is the forces of domination from the old order of the world which create chaos in our midst. It is the forces of domination which seek to divide us.

No, sisters and brothers, we cannot develop economically, nor socially, nor culturally, until we have removed these forces of domination. We will, rather, move towards decline and yet greater decline, if we ignore this fact and allow outside forces to continue their attempts to divide us, to sow diversion and deviation among us.

Look, I beg you, look at what is happening now to Cyprus, to Cambodia, to Vietnam! Look, too, at what is happening in what they call "Malaysia," where foreign bases are used against both the freedom fighters of North Kalimantan and against Indonesia. In all these cases, military bases, and sometimes economic institutions too, which were established by the forces trying to maintain the vested interests of the old order of the world, are being used against developing countries.

How can peaceful co-existence be applied in cases such as these? Ah, no! Peaceful co-existence is not a problem between powers of equal strength. Peaceful co-existence is a problem between powers of unequal strength, especially because the imperialist forces are using their strength to dominate the weaker developing countries.

In order to achieve the application of peaceful co-existence, the conditions for its practice must be laid down, just as Moscow and Washington laid down the conditions for the peaceful co-existence that now prevails between them. Peaceful co-existence cannot be imposed. I repeat, *peaceful co-existence cannot be imposed*. Peaceful co-existence needs a balance, an equilibrium of force. Peaceful co-existence is not an abstract. It is not a notion for artificial application regardless of everything else. Peaceful co-existence must be and always will be practiced in the concrete conditions of the balance of forces.

There will be peaceful co-existence between us, the developing countries, and the imperialist states only when we can face them with equal strength. And that equal strength we can obtain only through solidarity among us. Let there be no mistake about that! We have no alternative to solidarity.

And let us not suffer from the illusion that concentration upon economic development and the building of our military strength alone will bring us equal strength! No matter how deep our concentration upon economic and military development, no matter what our energies, we certainly will not even be able to neutralize the economic and military strength of imperialism!

It is true we have all learned much during our struggle for national independence. But, having gained that experience, let us not become self-complacent. Let us be realistic, and let us see things as they really are. Those experiences of ours, valuable, most valuable though they are, are not adequate, are often not even of the right kind to allow us individually to face this problem of the confrontation that still goes on and that still will go on, between our developing nationhoods and the old forces of imperialism.

In this struggle, we need to lean upon one another, we need to learn one another's experiences. Let us be alert, let us be quick to see the changing pattern of imperialist tactics. Let us not be behindhand and become deceived by those tactics and misled, so that we are divided among ourselves. Above all, we need to foster and to strengthen the solidarity among us. Let us not be deceived, let us not be misled. The struggle, yes, struggle, against imperialism in this present period of nation-building is as imperative for us as the struggle for liberation that led to our national independence.

Our non-alignment, as I said in Belgrade, "is active devotion to the lofty cause of independence, abiding peace, social justice, and the freedom to be free." Active devotion! Therefore, it is actively opposed to domination by the forces of the old order of the world which, above all, deny the freedom to be free, since this is the freedom which spells doom forever to those forces. It fights the domination by the forces of the old order of the world!

We have our work before us. We must chart a course to guide us through this turbulent period of transition in the world with the least possible suffering for humanity, in the shortest possible time. We must formulate principles which will guarantee the security of our developing countries.

We may never forget that we fight for all humanity. We may never forget the past sufferings of our people so that we lose sight of our original goal, and become deflected from our original course through the machinations of the forces of domination, which seek to destroy us in order to maintain themselves.

Well, then, strengthen the solidarity of the non-aligned countries! Strengthen the solidarity of all the new emerging forces which seek to build a new better world!

EXCERPT FROM ADDRESS BY
PRIME MINISTER
LAL BAHADUR SHASTRI OF INDIA

. . . The non-aligned nations have the supreme task to chalk out in the light of the latest developments in the world a program of action which should be followed in pursuit of their common objectives. The time has now come to formulate a positive program in furtherance of peace. The main elements in the program in our view should be the following five points:

1. Nuclear disarmament
2. Peaceful settlement of border disputes
3. Freedom from foreign domination, aggression, subversion and racial discrimination
4. Acceleration of economic development through international cooperation
5. Full support for the United Nations and its programs for peace and development

First and foremost, there is the program of nuclear disarmament. We note with satisfaction that there has been a measure of agreement, however limited, at the Geneva disarmament conference. When the conference resumes its sessions, we would all hope and wish for further progress, and we, the non-aligned countries, should continue to play a helpful role in promoting an agreement towards total nuclear disarmament. It is important to realize that a mere limitation of tests, a proclamation of certain areas as being free from nuclear weapons and any other limited measures of this character will not, and cannot, suffice to protect humanity from the horrors of a nuclear war. Nuclear disarmament must be total and complete and it is in that direction that we must move.

We cannot but express our serious concern at the fact that not all powers have agreed to subscribe to the partial test ban treaty. The non-aligned nations must take a clear and forthright attitude in calling upon all the nations of the world to accept the ban on nuclear tests and our full moral force must be brought to bear on those countries which still refuse to subscribe to the partial nuclear test ban treaty.

Many of those assembled here might recall how strongly the first non-aligned nations' conference at Belgrade felt on the subject of nuclear tests and how separate missions were sent to the U.S.A. and to the U.S.S.R. to persuade them to desist from further tests. With this background in mind, this conference should consider the recent disturbing indications which suggest that China is about to explode a nuclear device. I would propose that we might consider sending a special mission to persuade China to desist from developing nuclear weapons. I say this not because India and China have their differences today; these differences must sooner or later be resolved. But the threat to humanity from one more country having nuclear weapons at its disposal is a far more serious matter. We in India stand committed to use atomic energy only for peaceful purposes and even though, in a purely technical and scientific sense, we have the capability of developing nuclear weapons, our scientists and technicians are under firm orders not to make a single experiment, not to perfect a single device which is not needed for the peaceful uses of atomic energy. Despite all our differences, may I venture to take this opportunity of appealing through this conference to China to accept a similar discipline.

My second point relates to the peaceful settlement of border disputes. While the cold war has abated somewhat, yet all too often, fighting breaks out in different parts of the world because neighbors have boundary disputes. We should welcome the proposals made by Chairman Khrushchev and other heads of government on the renunciation of the use of force for solving territorial disputes or questions of frontiers. At the recent meeting of the Organization of African Unity, the African states have pledged themselves to respect borders existing on their achievement of national independence. This is a positive lead which must be followed and the principle should be made universal.

It is obvious that if this principle is to be successful, we must evolve other methods of settling such differences and disputes. Direct negotiations between the parties concerned would be the solution. As the late President Kennedy has so fittingly said, "While we should never negotiate out of fear, we should never fear to negotiate."

Quite often, the commencement of negotiations is hampered by one party or the other seeking to impose certain conditions. Negotiations to be real and fruitful must be free from all preconditions. Their basis must be the customary or traditional boundaries which may be in existence and not any new boundaries that may have been created by force of any kind. The non-aligned nations should declare their strong opposition to any changes brought about by the open use of force as well as by quiet penetration of borders or subversion of one kind or another. In this context, it would be relevant to recall the famous words used by Jawaharlal Nehru more than a decade ago: "Where freedom is menaced or justice is threatened or where aggression takes place, we cannot be and shall not be neutral."

Thirdly, both because of our past history and our own freedom struggle, we stand unequivocally for the emancipation of colonies and dependent countries. We strongly believe in theory as well as in practice in giving equal opportunities to all regardless of race, caste, creed or sex. We are entirely opposed to the doctrine of racialism wheresoever and in whatsoever form it may be practiced.

On this continent of Africa there unhappily continue quite a few areas which are still under the shackles of colonial rule. Portuguese oppression is continuing in Angola, Mozambique and so-called Portuguese Guinea. In Southern Rhodesia the white minority government seeks to impose its will on the majority. Here fortunately the recent meeting of the Commonwealth Prime Ministers held in London decided that no unilateral declaration of independence by the white settler community could be recognized. Over South-West Africa the illegal and alien rule of South Africa continues in defiance of world public opinion. We greet the freedom fighters from Angola and other oppressed territories and offer them our full support for the success of their heroic struggle for independence.

While we stand pledged to the right of self-determination for dependent territories under colonial rule, I would like to sound a note of caution. Self-determination is the right of any country that is dominated by another. But there can be no self-determination for different areas and regions within a sovereign and independent country, for this would lead only to fragmentation and disruption, and no country's integrity would be safe.

The hateful policies of apartheid and racial discrimination of the Union of South Africa are an affront to mankind. India severed her trade relations completely with South Africa at considerable loss to us in purely economic terms in 1946, and she has adhered firmly to this policy through all these years. How we wish more countries were able to observe and implement this policy! In fact, strict economic sanctions must be applied by the world community and there should be a complete and effective ban on the supply particularly of arms and oil. The struggle for defense of human values in South Africa must continue until it is crowned with success.

While racialism has to be strongly condemned, whether it is of the South African variety or any other, may I suggest to the non-aligned nations that sometimes it becomes essential to "look within." May I in that context say that we also have to make sure that no form of racialism is allowed to operate among the citizens of member countries. Discriminatory action against residents of a certain racial origin can also be harmful. Sometimes economic considerations are at the back of such steps, and certainly exploitation of any sort by any class or community of another is to be deplored. But care must be taken that any action initiated on economic grounds does not end in racial bias or discrimination. If any state or government faces special difficulties on account of persons living there who were originally from another country, then it is best that these are tackled after mutual discussion and consultation.

The program for economic development through international cooperation which is my fourth point is not—let me emphasize at the outset—a program for seeking more aid. It is basically a program of greater effort on the part of each developing country to mobilize its own resources. We want to stand on our own feet. If we are unable to do so straightaway, it is mainly because of the long period of political subjection which has sapped our resources and stifled our initiative. We, therefore, need help but the help we seek should be the minimum and not the maximum, and it should be directed towards making us independent of aid. In such a program we, the developing nations, must help ourselves and help each other even before we seek assistance from outside. Although we may be individually deficient in different things, through cooperation among ourselves, we can do a great deal for each other. We, in India, are trying our best to muster our technical and material resources to participate in a program of economic cooperation with other developing countries to whom we can be of assistance.

We are now in the middle of what is called the United Nations Development Decade. We have had a conference on trade and development in Geneva earlier this year. May I say that while these are important steps in the right direction, we are not satisfied with what has been done or promised so far. The target of economic growth which was set for the development decade by the United Nations is in need of an upward revision. The work done at Geneva needs to be carried forward on the lines indicated in the joint declaration of the seventy-seven developing countries made at the conclusion of the conference. Meanwhile, all states must agree to implement the recommendations embodied in the final act. The most important of these is the bringing into being of the new international institutions which have been envisaged. Unless the developing countries can expand and diversify their export trade, unless the transfer of capital from the developed to developing countries on satisfactory terms can be accelerated, economic progress will not attain a pace compatible with peace and freedom.

My fifth and last point relates to the support which all of us must give to the United Nations in the pursuit of the policies to which I have just referred. We are all members of the United Nations and if we meet and confer apart, we do so only with a view to strengthen the United Nations as an organization and to carry its objectives forward. The United Nations has been moving steadily in the direction of universality of membership. The major exception is China which is still not a member. Although we have our differences with China, we have always supported and still support her admission to the United Nations. Furthermore, as the countries which are still under colonial regimes of one kind or other attain their independence, we would hope to see every part of the globe represented through a government of its own choice in the United Nations.

The United Nations as a whole has given support to the policies and programs of peace, freedom and progress, which have been engaging our attention here. We should support it not merely in words but in action. It is on the non-aligned nations that the brunt of supplying forces for the peace-keeping operations falls. India has on many occasions placed her armed forces at the disposal of the United Nations for keeping the peace. It is, therefore, for the non-aligned nations to take the greatest interest in how these operations are entered into, organized, financed and manned.

Despite the progress which has been made, we cannot shut our eyes to the fact that all is not well with the world. In South and Southeast Asia there is an atmosphere of conflict and tension. The long travail of Vietnam and Laos continues. Cyprus has not yet been freed from its sufferings. The situation in the Congo remains uncertain and unstable. In the Caribbean area there are tensions and frictions. On our own northern borders, despite our acceptance of the proposals made by the non-aligned powers assembled at Colombo, we have been unable to get a friendly response from China. But we must continue to strive for peace, to resolve all differences through peaceful methods by conciliation, as distinct from confrontation, and by trust instead of suspicion.

THE PROGRAM FOR PEACE AND INTERNATIONAL COOPERATION

The second conference of heads of state or government of the following non-aligned countries:

Afghanistan, Algeria, Angola, Burma, Burundi, Cambodia, Cameroon, Central African Republic, Ceylon, Chad, Congo (Brazzaville), Cuba, Cyprus, Dahomey, Ethiopia, Ghana, Guinea, India, Indonesia, Iraq, Islamic Republic of Mauritania, Jordan, Kenya, Kuwait, Laos, Lebanon, Liberia, Libya, Malawi, Mali, Morocco, Nepal, Nigeria, Saudi Arabia, Senegal, Sierra Leone, Somalia, Sudan, Syria, Togo, Tunisia, Uganda, United Arab Republic, United Republic of Tanganyika and Zanzibar, Yemen, Yugoslavia and Zambia was held in Cairo from October 5 to 10, 1964.

The following countries:

Argentina, Bolivia, Brazil, Chile, Finland, Jamaica, Mexico, Trinidad and Tobago, Uruguay and Venezuela were represented by observers.

The Secretary-General of the Organization of African Unity and the Secretary-General of the League of Arab States were present as observers.

The conference undertook an analysis of the international situation with a view to making an effective contribution to the solution of the major problems which are of concern to mankind in view of their effects on peace and security in the world.

To this end, and on the basis of the principles embodied in the Belgrade declaration of September, 1961, the heads of state or government of the above-mentioned countries proceeded, in an amicable, frank and fraternal atmosphere, to hold detailed discussions and an exchange of views on the present state of international relations and the predominant trends in the modern world. The heads of state or government of the participating countries note with satisfaction that nearly half of the independent countries of the world have participated in this second non-aligned conference.

The conference also notes with satisfaction the growing interest and confidence displayed by peoples still under foreign domination, and by those whose rights and sovereignty are being violated by imperialism and neo-colonialism, in the highly positive role which the non-aligned countries are called upon to play in the settlement of international problems or disputes.

The conference expresses satisfaction at the favorable reaction throughout the world to this second meeting of non-aligned countries. This emphasizes the rightness, efficacy and vigor of the policy of non-alignment, and its constructive role in the maintenance and consolidation of international peace and security.

The principles of non-alignment, thanks to the confidence they inspire in the world, are becoming an increasingly dynamic and powerful force for the promotion of peace and the welfare of mankind.

The participating heads of state or government note with satisfaction that, thanks to the combined efforts of the forces of freedom, peace and progress, this second non-aligned conference is being held at a time when the international situation has improved as compared with that which existed between the two power blocs at the time of the historic Belgrade conference. The heads of state or government of the non-aligned countries are well aware, however, that, despite the present improvement in international relations, and notwithstanding the conclusion and signature of the Treaty of Moscow, sources of tension still exist in many parts of the world.

This situation shows that the forces of imperialism are

still powerful and that they do not hesitate to resort to the use of force to defend their interests and maintain their privileges.

This policy, if not firmly resisted by the forces of freedom and peace, is likely to jeopardize the improvement in the international situation and the lessening of tension which has occurred, and to constitute a threat to world peace.

The policy of active peaceful co-existence is an indivisible whole. It cannot be applied partially, in accordance with special interests and criteria.

Important changes have also taken place within the Eastern and Western blocs, and this new phenomenon should be taken into account in the objective assessment of the current international situation.

The conference notes with satisfaction that the movements of national liberation are engaged, in different regions of the world, in a heroic struggle against neo-colonialism and the practices of apartheid and racial discrimination. This struggle forms part of the common striving towards freedom, justice and peace.

The conference reaffirms that interference by economically developed foreign states in the internal affairs of newly independent, developing countries and the existence of territories which are still dependent constitute a standing threat to peace and security.

The heads of state or government of the non-aligned countries, while appreciative of the efforts which resulted in the holding of the United Nations Conference on Trade and Development, and mindful of the results of that conference, nevertheless note that much ground still remains to be covered to eliminate existing inequalities in the relationship between industrialized and developing countries.

The heads of state or government of the non-aligned countries, while declaring their determination to contribute towards the establishment of just and lasting peace in the world, affirm that the preservation of peace and the promotion of the well-being of peoples are a collective responsibility deriving from the natural aspirations of mankind to live in a better world.

The heads of state or government have arrived in their deliberations at a common understanding of the various problems with which the world is now faced, and a common approach to them. Reaffirming the basic principles of the declaration of Belgrade, they express their agreement upon the following points:

I   Concerted action for the liberation of the countries still dependent; elimination of colonialism, neo-colonialism and imperialism

The heads of state or government of the non-aligned countries declare that lasting world peace cannot be realized so long as unjust conditions prevail and peoples under foreign domination continue to be deprived of their fundamental right to freedom, independence and self-determination.

Imperialism, colonialism and neo-colonialism constitute a basic source of international tension and conflict because they endanger world peace and security. The participants in the conference deplore that the declaration of the United Nations on the granting of independence to colonial countries and peoples has not been implemented everywhere and call for the unconditional, complete and final abolition of colonialism now.

At present a particular cause of concern is the military or other assistance extended to certain countries to enable them to perpetuate by force colonialist and neo-colonialist situations which are contrary to the spirit of the Charter of the United Nations.

The exploitation by colonialist forces of the difficulties and problems of recently liberated or developing countries, interference in the internal affairs of these states, and colonialist attempts to maintain unequal relationships, particularly in the economic field, constitute serious dangers to these young countries. Colonialism and neo-colonialism have many forms and manifestations.

Imperialism uses many devices to impose its will on independent nations. Economic pressure and domination, interference, racial discrimination, subversion, intervention and the threat of force are neo-colonialist devices against which the newly independent nations have to defend themselves. The conference condemns all colonialist, neo-colonialist and imperialist policies applied in various parts of the world.

Deeply concerned at the rapidly deteriorating situation in the Congo, the participants:

1) support all the efforts being made by the Organization of African Unity to bring peace and harmony speedily to that country;

2) urge the ad hoc commission of the Organization of African Unity to shirk no effort in the attempt to achieve national reconciliation in the Congo, and to eliminate the existing tension between that country and the Republic of the Congo (Brazzaville) and the Kingdom of Burundi;

3) appeal to the Congolese government and to all combatants to cease hostilities immediately and to seek, with the help of the Organization of African Unity, a solution permitting national reconciliation and the restoration of order and peace;

4) urgently appeal to all foreign powers at present interfering in the internal affairs of the Democratic Republic of the Congo, particularly those engaged in military intervention in that country, to cease such interference, which infringes the interests and sovereignty of the Congolese people and constitutes a threat to neighboring countries;

5) affirm their full support for the efforts being made to this end by the Organization of African Unity's ad hoc commission of good offices in the Congo;

6) call upon the government of the Democratic Republic

of the Congo to discontinue the recruitment of mercenaries immediately and to expel all mercenaries of whatever origin who are already in the Congo, in order to facilitate an African solution.

The newly independent countries have, like all other countries, the right of sovereign disposal in regard to their natural resources, and the right to utilize these resources as they deem appropriate in the interest of their peoples, without outside interference.

The process of liberation is irresistible and irreversible. Colonized peoples may legitimately resort to arms to secure the full exercise of their right to self-determination and independence if the colonial powers persist in opposing their natural aspirations.

The participants in the conference undertake to work unremittingly to eradicate all vestiges of colonialism, and to combine all their efforts to render all necessary aid and support, whether moral, political or material, to the peoples struggling against colonialism and neo-colonialism. The participating countries recognize the nationalist movements of the peoples which are struggling to free themselves from colonial domination as being authentic representatives of the colonial peoples, and urgently call upon the colonial powers to negotiate with their leaders.

Portugal continues to hold in bondage by repression, persecution and force, in Angola, Mozambique, so-called Portuguese Guinea and the other Portuguese colonies in Africa and Asia, millions of people who have been suffering far too long under the foreign yoke. The conference declares its determination to ensure that the peoples of these territories accede immediately to independence without any conditions or reservations.

The conference condemns the government of Portugal for its obstinate refusal to recognize the inalienable right of the peoples of those territories to self-determination and independence in accordance with the Charter of the United Nations and the Declaration on the Granting of Independence to Colonial Countries and Peoples.

The conference:

1) urges the participating countries to afford all necessary material support—financial and military—to the freedom fighters in the territories under Portuguese colonial rule;

2) takes the view that support should be given to the Revolutionary Government of Angola in exile and to the nationalist movements struggling for the independence of the Portuguese colonies and assistance to the special bureau set up by the OAU in regard to the application of sanctions against Portugal;

3) calls upon all participating states to break off diplomatic and consular relations with the government of Portugal and to take effective measures to suspend all trade and economic relations with Portugal;

4) calls upon the participating countries to take all measures to compel Portugal to carry out the decisions of the General Assembly of the United Nations;

5) addresses an urgent appeal to the powers which are extending military aid and assistance to Portugal to withdraw such aid and assistance.

The countries participating in the conference condemn the policy of the racist minority regime in Southern Rhodesia, which continues to defy the Charter and the resolutions of the United Nations in that it denies fundamental freedoms to the people by acts of repression and terror.

The participating countries urge all states not to recognize the independence of Southern Rhodesia if proclaimed under the rule of the racist minority, and instead to give favorable consideration to according recognition to an African nationalist government in exile, should such a government be set up. To this effect, the conference states its opposition to the sham consultation through tribal chiefs envisaged by the present minority government of Southern Rhodesia.

The conference deplores the British government's failure to implement the various resolutions of the United Nations relating to Southern Rhodesia and calls upon the United Kingdom to convene immediately a constitutional conference, to which all political groups in Southern Rhodesia would be invited, for the purpose of preparing a new constitution based on the "one man, one vote" principle, instituting universal suffrage, and ensuring majority rule.

The conference urges the government of the United Kingdom to call for the immediate release of all political prisoners and detainees in Southern Rhodesia.

The conference reaffirms the inalienable right of the people of South-West Africa to self-determination and independence and condemns the government of South Africa for its persistent refusal to cooperate with the United Nations in the implementation of the pertinent resolutions of the General Assembly.

It urges all states to refrain from supplying in any manner or form any arms or military equipment or petroleum products to South Africa, and to implement the resolutions of the United Nations.

The conference recommends that the United Nations should guarantee the territorial integrity of dependent territories for their speedy accession to independence and for the subsequent safeguarding of their sovereignty.

The participants in the conference call upon the French government to take the necessary steps to enable French Somaliland to become free and independent in accordance with paragraph 5 of Resolution 1514 (XV) of the United Nations.

The conference appeals to all participating countries to lend support and assistance to the liberation committee of the Organization of African Unity.

The conference condemns the imperialistic policy pursued in the Middle East and, in conformity with the Charter of the United Nations, decides to:

1) endorse the full restoration of all the rights of the Arab people of Palestine to their homeland, and their inalienable right to self-determination;

2) declare their full support to the Arab people of Palestine in their struggle for liberation from colonialism and racism.

The conference condemns the continued refusal of the United Kingdom government to implement the United Nations resolutions on Aden and the Protectorates, providing for the free exercise by the peoples of the territory of their right to self-determination and calling for the liquidation of the British military base in Aden and the withdrawal of British troops from the territory.

The conference fully supports the struggle of the people of Aden and the Protectorates and urges the immediate implementation of the resolutions of the United Nations which are based on the expressed wishes of the people of the territory.

The countries participating in the conference condemn the continued armed action waged by British colonialism against the people of Oman who are fighting to attain their freedom.

The conference recommends that all necessary political, moral and material assistance be rendered to the liberation movements of these territories in their struggle against colonial rule.

The conference condemns the manifestations of colonialism and neo-colonialism in Latin America and declares itself in favor of the implementation in that region of the right of peoples to self-determination and independence.

Basing itself on this principle, the conference deplores the delay in granting full independence to British Guiana and requests the United Kingdom to grant independence speedily to that country. It notes with regret that Martinique, Guadeloupe and other Caribbean islands are still not self-governing. It draws the attention of the ad hoc de-colonization commission of the United Nations to the case of Puerto Rico and calls upon that commission to consider the situation of these territories in the light of Resolution 1514 (XV) of the United Nations.

II   Respect for the right of peoples to self-determination and condemnation of the use of force against the exercise of this right

The conference solemnly reaffirms the right of peoples to self-determination and to make their own destiny.

It stresses that this right constitutes one of the essential principles of the United Nations Charter, that it was laid down also in the Charter of the Organization of African Unity, and that the conferences of Bandung and Belgrade demanded that it should be respected, and in particular insisted that it should be effectively exercised.

The conference notes that this right is still violated or its exercise denied in many regions of the world and results in a continued increase of tension and the extension of the areas of war.

The conference denounces the attitude of those powers which oppose the exercise of the right of peoples to self-determination.

It condemns the use of force, and all forms of intimidation, interference and intervention which are aimed at preventing the exercise of this right.

III   Racial discrimination and the policy of apartheid

The heads of state or government declare that racial discrimination—and particularly its most odious manifestation, apartheid—constitutes a violation of the Universal Declaration of Human Rights and of the principle of the equality of peoples. Accordingly, all governments still persisting in the practice of racial discrimination should be completely ostracized until they have abandoned their unjust and inhuman policies. In particular the governments and peoples represented at this conference have decided that they will not tolerate much longer the presence of the Republic of South Africa in the community of nations. The inhuman racial policies of South Africa constitute a threat to international peace and security. All countries interested in peace must therefore do everything in their power to ensure that liberty and fundamental freedoms are secured to the people of South Africa.

The heads of state or government solemnly affirm their absolute respect for the right of ethnic or religious minorities to protection in particular against the crimes of genocide or any other violation of a fundamental human right.

SANCTIONS AGAINST THE REPUBLIC OF SOUTH AFRICA

1) The conference regrets to note that the Pretoria government's obstinacy in defying the conscience of mankind has been strengthened by the refusal of its friends and allies, particularly some major powers, to implement United Nations resolutions concerning sanctions against South Africa.

2) The conference therefore:

a) calls upon all states to boycott all South African goods and to refrain from exporting goods, especially arms, ammunition, oil and minerals to South Africa;

b) calls upon all states which have not yet done so to break off diplomatic, consular and other relations with South Africa;

c) requests the governments represented at this conference to deny airport and overflying facilities to aircraft and port facilities to ships proceeding to and from South Africa, and to discontinue all road or railway traffic with that country;

d) demands the release of all persons imprisoned, interned or subjected to other restrictions on account of their opposition to the policy of apartheid;

c) invites all countries to give their support to the special bureau set up by the Organization of African Unity for the application of sanctions against South Africa.

IV Peaceful co-existence and the codification of its principles by the United Nations

Considering the principles proclaimed at Bandung in 1955, Resolution 1514 (XV) adopted by the United Nations in 1960, the declaration of the Belgrade conference, the Charter of the Organization of African Unity, and numerous joint declarations by heads of state or government on peaceful co-existence;

Reaffirming their deep conviction that, in present circumstances, mankind must regard peaceful co-existence as the only way to strengthen world peace, which must be based on freedom, equality and justice between peoples within a new framework of peaceful and harmonious relations between the states and nations of the world;

Considering the fact that the principle of peaceful co-existence is based on the right of all peoples to be free and to choose their own political, economic and social systems according to their own national identity and their ideals, and is opposed to any form of foreign domination;

Convinced also that peaceful co-existence cannot be fully achieved throughout the world without the abolition of imperialism, colonialism and neo-colonialism;

Deeply convinced that the absolute prohibition of the threat or use of force, direct or disguised, the renunciation of all forms of coercion in international relations, the abolition of relations of inequality and the promotion of international cooperation with a view to accelerating economic, social and cultural development, are necessary conditions for safeguarding peace and achieving the general advancement of mankind,

The heads of state or government solemnly proclaim the following fundamental principles of peaceful co-existence:

1. The right to complete independence, which is an inalienable right, must be recognized immediately and unconditionally as pertaining to all peoples, in conformity with the Charter and resolutions of the United Nations General Assembly; it is incumbent upon all states to respect this right and facilitate its exercise.

2. The right to self-determination, which is an inalienable right, must be recognized as pertaining to all peoples; accordingly, all nations and peoples have the right to determine their political status and freely pursue their economic, social and cultural development without intimidation or hindrance.

3. Peaceful co-existence between states with differing social and political systems is both possible and necessary; it favors the creation of good-neighborly relations between states with a view to the establishment of lasting peace and general well-being, free from domination and exploitation.

4. The sovereign equality of states must be recognized and respected. It includes the right of all peoples to the free exploitation of their natural resources.

5. States must abstain from all use of threat or force directed against the territorial integrity and political independence of other states; a situation brought about by the threat or use of force shall not be recognized, and in particular the established frontiers of states shall be inviolable. Accordingly, every state must abstain from interfering in the affairs of other states, whether openly, or insidiously, or by means of subversion and the various forms of political, economic and military pressure. Frontier disputes shall be settled by peaceful means.

6. All states shall respect the fundamental rights and freedoms of the human person and the equality of all nations and races.

7. All international conflicts must be settled by peaceful means, in a spirit of mutual understanding and on the basis of equality and sovereignty, in such a manner that justice and legitimate rights are not impaired; all states must apply themselves to promoting and strengthening measures designed to diminish international tension and achieve general and complete disarmament.

8. All states must cooperate with a view to accelerating economic development in the world, and particularly in the developing countries. This cooperation, which must be aimed at narrowing the gap, at present widening, between the levels of living in the developing and developed countries respectively, is essential to the maintenance of a lasting peace.

9. States shall meet their international obligations in good faith in conformity with the principles and purposes of the United Nations.

The conference recommends to the General Assembly of the United Nations to adopt, on the occasion of its twentieth anniversary, a declaration on the principles of peaceful coexistence. This declaration will constitute an important step towards the codification of these principles.

V Respect for the sovereignty of states and their territorial integrity; problems of divided nations

1) The conference of heads of state or government proclaims its full adherence to the fundamental principle of international relations, in accordance with which the sovereignty and territorial integrity of all states, great and small, are inviolable and must be respected.

2) The countries participating in the conference, having for the most part achieved their national independence after years of struggle, reaffirm their determination to oppose by every means in their power any attempt to compromise their sovereignty or violate their territorial integrity. They pledge themselves to respect frontiers as they existed when the

states gained independence; nevertheless, parts of territories taken away by occupying powers or converted into autonomous bases for their own benefit at the time of independence must be given back to the country concerned.

3) The conference solemnly reaffirms the right of all peoples to adopt the form of government they consider best suited to their development.

4) The conference considers that one of the causes of international tension lies in the problem of divided nations. It expresses its entire sympathy with the peoples of such countries and upholds their desire to achieve unity. It exhorts the countries concerned to seek a just and lasting solution in order to achieve the unification of their territories by peaceful methods without outside interference or pressure. It considers that the resort to threat or force can lead to no satisfactory settlement, cannot do otherwise than jeopardize international security.

Concerned by the situation existing with regard to Cyprus, the conference calls upon all states in conformity with their obligations under the Charter of the United Nations, and in particular under article 2, paragraph 4, to respect the sovereignty, unity, independence and territorial integrity of Cyprus and to refrain from any threat or use of force or intervention directed against Cyprus and from any efforts to impose upon Cyprus unjust solutions unacceptable to the people of Cyprus.

Cyprus, as an equal member of the United Nations, is entitled to and should enjoy unrestricted and unfettered sovereignty and independence, allowing its people to determine freely, and without any foreign intervention or interference, the political future of the country, in accordance with the Charter of the United Nations.

The conference, considering that foreign pressure and intervention to impose changes in the political, economic and social system chosen by a country are contrary to the principles of international law and peaceful co-existence, requests the Government of the United States of America to lift the commercial and economic blockade applied against Cuba.

The conference takes note of the readiness of the Cuban government to settle its differences with the United States on an equal footing, and invites these two governments to enter into negotiations to this end and in conformity with the principles of peaceful co-existence and international cooperation.

Taking into account the principles set forth above and with a view to restoring peace and stability in the Indochina peninsula, the conference appeals to the powers which participated in the Geneva conferences of 1954 and 1962:

1) to abstain from any action likely to aggravate the situation which is already tense in the peninsula;

2) to terminate all foreign interference in the internal affairs of the countries of that region;

3) to convene urgently a new Geneva conference on Indochina with a view to seeking a satisfactory political solution for the peaceful settlement of the problems arising in that part of the world, namely:

> a) ensuring the strict application of the 1962 agreements on Laos;
>
> b) recognizing and guaranteeing the neutrality and territorial integrity of Cambodia;
>
> c) ensuring the strict application of the 1954 Geneva Agreement on Vietnam, and finding a political solution to the problem in accordance with the legitimate aspirations of the Vietnamese people to freedom, peace and independence.

VI   Settlement of disputes without threat or use of force in accordance with the principles of the United Nations Charter

1) As the use of force may take a number of forms, military, political and economic, the participating countries deem

it essential to reaffirm the principle that all states shall refrain in their international relations from the threat or use of force against the territorial integrity or political independence of any state, or in any other manner inconsistent with the purposes of the Charter of the United Nations.

2) They consider that disputes between states should be settled by peaceful means in accordance with the Charter on the basis of sovereign equality and justice.

3) The participating countries are convinced of the necessity of exerting all international efforts to find solutions to all situations which threaten international peace or impair friendly relations among nations.

4) The participating countries gave special attention to the problems of frontiers which may threaten international peace or disturb friendly relations among states, and are convinced that in order to settle such problems, all states should resort to negotiation, mediation or arbitration or other peaceful means set forth in the United Nations Charter in conformity with the legitimate rights of all peoples.

5) The conference considers that disputes between neighboring states must be settled peacefully in a spirit of mutual understanding, without foreign intervention or interference.

VII   General and complete disarmament; peaceful use of atomic energy; prohibition of all nuclear weapon tests; establishment of nuclear-free zones; prevention of dissemination of nuclear weapons and abolition of all nuclear weapons

The conference emphasizes the paramount importance of disarmament as one of the basic problems of the contemporary world, and stresses the necessity of reaching immediate and practical solutions which would free mankind from the danger of war and from a sense of insecurity.

The conference notes with concern that the continuing

arms race and the tremendous advances that have been made in the production of weapons of mass destruction and their stockpiling threaten the world with armed conflict and annihilation. The conference urges the great powers to take new and urgent steps towards achieving general and complete disarmament under strict and effective international control.

The conference regrets that despite the efforts of the members of the eighteen-nation committee on disarmament, and in particular those of the non-aligned countries, the results have not been satisfactory. It urges the great powers, in collaboration with the other members of that committee, to renew their efforts with determination with a view to the rapid conclusion of an agreement on general and complete disarmament.

The conference calls upon all states to accede to the Moscow treaty partially banning the testing of nuclear weapons, and to abide by its provisions in the interests of peace and the welfare of humanity.

The conference urges the extension of the Moscow treaty so as to include underground tests, and the discontinuance of such tests pending the extension of the agreement.

The conference urges the speedy conclusion of agreements on various other partial and collateral measures of disarmament proposed by the members of the eighteen-nation committee on disarmament.

The conference appeals to the great powers to take the lead in giving effect to decisive and immediate measures which would make possible substantial reductions in their military budgets.

The conference requests the great powers to abstain from all policies conducive to the dissemination of nuclear weapons and their by-products among those states which do not at present possess them. It underlines the great danger in the dissemination of nuclear weapons and urges all states, particularly those possessing nuclear weapons, to conclude non-dissemination agreements and to agree on measures providing for the gradual liquidation of the existing stockpiles of nuclear weapons.

As part of these efforts, the heads of state or government declare their own readiness not to produce, acquire or test any nuclear weapons, and call on all countries including those who have not subscribed to the Moscow treaty to enter into a similar undertaking and to take the necessary steps to prevent their territories, ports and airfields from being used by nuclear powers for the deployment or disposition of nuclear weapons. This undertaking should be the subject of a treaty to be concluded in an international conference convened under the auspices of the United Nations and open to accession by all states. The conference further calls upon all nuclear powers to observe the spirit of this declaration.

The conference welcomes the agreement of the great powers not to orbit in outer space nuclear or other weapons of mass destruction and expresses its conviction that it is necessary to conclude an international treaty prohibiting the utilization of outer space for military purposes. The conference urges full international cooperation in the peaceful uses of outer space.

The conference requests those states which have succeeded in exploring outer space to exchange and disseminate information related to the research they have carried out in this field, so that scientific progress for the peaceful utilization of outer space be of common benefit to all. The conference is of the view that for this purpose an international conference should be convened at an appropriate time.

The conference considers that the declaration by African states regarding the denuclearization of Africa, the aspirations of the Latin American countries to denuclearize their continent and the various proposals pertaining to the denuclearization of areas in Europe and Asia are steps in the right direction because they assist in consolidating international peace and security and lessening international tensions.

The conference recommends the establishment of denuclearized zones covering these and other areas and the oceans of the world, particularly those which have been hitherto free from nuclear weapons, in accordance with the desires expressed by the states and peoples concerned.

The conference also requests the nuclear powers to respect these denuclearized zones.

The conference is convinced that the convening of a world disarmament conference under the auspices of the United Nations, to which all countries would be invited, would provide powerful support to the efforts which are being made to set in motion the process of disarmament and for securing the further and steady development of this process.

The conference therefore urges the participating countries to take, at the forthcoming General Assembly of the United Nations, all the necessary steps for the holding of such a conference and of any other special conference for the conclusion of special agreements on certain measures of disarmament.

The conference urges all nations to join in the cooperative development of the peaceful use of atomic energy for the benefit of all mankind; and in particular, to study the development of atomic power and other technical aspects in which international cooperation might be most effectively accomplished through the free flow of such scientific information.

VIII Military pacts, foreign troops and bases

The conference reiterates its conviction that the existence of military blocs, great power alliances and pacts arising therefrom has accentuated the cold war and heightened international tensions. The non-aligned countries are therefore opposed to taking part in such pacts and alliances.

The conference considers the maintenance or future establishment of foreign military bases and the stationing of foreign troops on the territories of other countries against the expressed will of those countries as a gross violation of the sovereignty of states and as a threat to freedom and international peace. It furthermore considers as particularly indefensible the existence or future establishment of bases in dependent territories which could be used for the maintenance of colonialism or for other purposes.

Noting with concern that foreign military bases are in practice a means of bringing pressure on nations and retarding their emancipation and development, based on their own ideological, political, economic and cultural ideas, the conference declares its full support to the countries which are seeking to secure the evacuation of foreign bases on their territory and calls upon all states maintaining troops and bases in other countries to remove them forthwith.

The conference considers that the maintenance at Guantanamo (Cuba) of a military base of the United States of America, in defiance of the will of the government and people of Cuba and in defiance of the provisions embodied in the declaration of the Belgrade conference, constitutes a violation of Cuba's sovereignty and territorial integrity.

Noting that the Cuban government expresses its readiness to settle its dispute over the base of Guantanamo with the United States on an equal footing, the conference urges the United States government to negotiate the evacuation of this base with the Cuban government.

The conference condemns the expressed intention of imperialist powers to establish bases in the Indian Ocean, as a calculated attempt to intimidate the emerging countries of Africa and Asia and an unwarranted extension of the policy of neo-colonialism and imperialism.

The conference also recommends the elimination of the foreign bases in Cyprus and the withdrawal of foreign troops from this country, except for those stationed there by virtue of United Nations resolutions.

IX   The United Nations: its role in international affairs, implementation of its resolutions and amendment of its Charter

The participating countries declare:

The United Nations Organization was established to promote international peace and security, to develop international understanding and cooperation, to safeguard human rights and fundamental freedom and to achieve all the purposes of the Charter. In order to be an effective instrument, the United Nations Organization must be open to all the states of the world. It is particularly necessary that countries still under colonial domination should attain independence without delay and take their rightful place in the community of nations.

It is essential for the effective functioning of the United Nations that all nations should observe its fundamental principles of peaceful co-existence, cooperation, renunciation of the threat or the use of force, freedom and equality without discrimination on grounds of race, sex, language or religion.

The influence and effectiveness of the United Nations also depends upon equitable representation of different geographical regions in the various organs of the United Nations and in the service of the United Nations.

The conference notes with satisfaction that with Resolution 1991 (XVIII), the General Assembly has taken the initial positive step towards transformation of the structure of the United Nations in keeping with its increased membership and the necessity to ensure a broader participation of states in the work of its organs. It appeals to all members of the United Nations to ratify as speedily as possible the amendments to the Charter adopted at the eighteenth session of the General Assembly.

The conference recognizes the paramount importance of the United Nations and the necessity of enabling it to carry out the functions entrusted to it to preserve international co-operation among states.

To this end, the non-aligned countries should consult one another at the foreign minister or head of delegation level at each session of the United Nations.

The conference stresses the need to adapt the Charter to the dynamic changes and evolution of international conditions.

The conference expresses the hope that the heads of state or government of the member states of the United Nations will attend the regular session of the General Assembly on the occasion of the twentieth anniversary of the organization.

Recalling the recommendation of the Belgrade conference, the conference asks the General Assembly of the United Nations to restore the rights of the People's Republic of China and to recognize the representatives of its government as the only legitimate representatives of China in the United Nations.

The conference recommends to the member states of the United Nations to respect the resolutions of the United Nations and to render all assistance necessary for the organization to fulfill its role in maintaining international peace and security.

X   Economic development and cooperation

The heads of state or government participating in this conference,

Convinced that peace must rest on a sound and solid economic foundation,

that the persistence of poverty poses a threat to world peace and prosperity,

that economic emancipation is an essential element in the struggle for the elimination of political domination,

that respect for the right of peoples and nations to

control and dispose freely of their national wealth and resources is vital for their economic development;

Conscious that participating states have a special responsibility to do their utmost to break through the barrier
of underdevelopment;

Believing that economic development is an obligation of
the whole international community,

that it is the duty of all countries to contribute to the
rapid evolution of a new and just economic order under
which all nations can live without fear or want or despair
and rise to their full stature in the family of nations,

that the structure of world economy and the existing international institutions of international trade and development have failed either to reduce the disparity in the per
capita income of the peoples in developing and developed
countries or to promote international action to rectify serious
and growing imbalances between developed and developing
countries;

Emphasizing the imperative need to amplify and intensify international cooperation based on equality, and consistent with the needs of accelerated economic development;

Noting that as a result of the proposals adopted at Bel-
grade in 1961 and elaborated in Cairo in 1962, the United
Nations Conference on Trade and Development met in
Geneva in 1964;

Considering that while the Geneva conference marks the
first step in the evolution of a new international economic
policy for development and offers a sound basis for progress
in the future, the results achieved were neither adequate for,
nor commensurate with, the essential requirements of developing countries;

Support the joint declaration of the seventy-seven developing countries made at the conclusion of that conference, and PLEDGE the cooperation of the participating
states to the strengthening of their solidarity;

Urge upon all states to implement on an urgent basis the

recommendations contained in the final act of the United Nations Conference on Trade and Development and in particular to cooperate in bringing into existence as early as possible the new international institutions proposed therein, so that the problems of trade and economic development may be more effectively and speedily resolved;

Consider that democratic procedures, which afford no position of privilege, are as essential in the economic as in the political sphere;

that a new international division of labor is needed to hasten the industrialization of developing countries and the modernization of their agriculture, so as to enable them to strengthen their domestic economies and diversify their export trade,

that discriminatory measures of any kind taken against developing countries on the grounds of different socio-economic systems are contrary to the spirit of the United Nations Charter and constitute a threat to the free flow of trade and to peace and should be eliminated;

Affirm that the practice of the inhuman policy of apartheid or racial discrimination in any part of the world should be eliminated by every possible means, including economic sanctions;

Recommend that the target of economic growth set for the development decade by the United Nations should be revised upwards,

that the amount of capital transferred to developing countries and the terms and conditions governing the transfer should be extended and improved without political commitments, so as to reinforce the efforts of these countries to build self-reliant economies.

that a program of action should be developed to increase the income in foreign exchange of developing countries and, in particular, to provide access for primary products from developing countries to the markets of industrialized countries, on an equitable basis and for manufactured goods from developing countries on a preferential basis,

that the establishment of a specialized agency for industrial development should be expedited,

that members of regional economic groupings should do their utmost to ensure that economic integration helps to promote the increase of imports from the developing countries either individually or collectively,

that the recommendation of the United Nations Conference on Trade and Development to convene a conference of plenipotentiaries to adopt an international convention to ensure the right of landlocked countries to free transit and access to the sea be implemented by the United Nations early next year, and that the principles of economic cooperation adopted by the United Nations Conference on Trade and Development in relation to the transit trade of landlocked countries be given consideration;

Call upon participating countries to concert measures to bring about closer economic relations among the developing countries on a basis of equality, mutual benefit and mutual assistance, bearing in mind the obligations of all developing countries to accord favorable consideration to the expansion of their reciprocal trade, to unite against all forms of economic exploitation and to strengthen mutual consultation;

Call upon the members of the seventy-seven developing countries who worked closely together at the United Nations Conference on Trade and Development of 1964 in Geneva to consult together during the next session of the General Assembly of the United Nations in order to consolidate their efforts and harmonize their policies in time for the next conference on trade and development in 1966;

Convinced that progress towards disarmament increases the resources available for economic development,

support proposals for the diversion of resources now employed on armaments to the development of underdeveloped parts of the world and to the promotion of the prosperity of mankind.

XI Cultural, scientific and educational cooperation and consolidation of the international and regional organizations working for this purpose

The heads of state or government participating in the conference,

Considering that the political, economic, social and cultural problems of mankind are so interrelated as to demand concerted action;

Considering that cooperation in the fields of culture, education and science is necessary for the deepening of human understanding, for the consolidation of freedom, justice and peace and for progress and development;

Bearing in mind that political liberation, social emancipation and scientific advancement have effected fundamental changes in the minds and lives of men;

Recognizing that culture helps to widen the mind and enrich life; that all human cultures have their special values and can contribute to the general progress; that many cultures were suppressed and cultural relations interrupted under colonial domination; that international understanding and progress require a revival and rehabilitation of these cultures, a free expression of their identity and national character and a deeper mutual appreciation of their values so as to enrich the common cultural heritage of man;

Considering that education is a basic need for the advancement of humanity and that science not only adds to the wealth and welfare of nations but also adds new values to civilization;

Appreciating the work of the international and regional organizations in the promotion of educational, scientific and cultural cooperation among nations;

Believing that such cooperation among nations in the

educational, scientific and cultural fields should be strengthened and expanded;

Recommend that international cooperation in education should be promoted in order to secure a fair opportunity for education to every person in every part of the world, to extend educational assistance to develop mutual understanding and appreciation of the different cultures and ways of life through the proper teaching of civics, and to promote international understanding through the teaching of the principles of the United Nations at various levels of education;

Propose that a free and more systematic exchange of scientific information be encouraged and intensified and, in particular, call on the advanced countries to share with developing countries their scientific knowledge and technical knowledge so that the advantages of scientific and technological advance can be applied to the promotion of economic development;

Urge all states to adopt in their legislation the principles embodied in the United Nations Declaration of Human Rights;

Agree that participating countries should adopt measures to strengthen their ties with one another in the fields of education, science and culture;

Express their determination to help consolidate and strengthen the international and regional organizations working in this direction.

The Lusaka Conference

SEPTEMBER 8–10, 1970

OPENING ADDRESS BY PRESIDENT KENNETH D. KAUNDA OF ZAMBIA

In the name of Almighty God, I declare open this Third Conference of Heads of State and Government of the Non-Aligned Nations.

May I now ask you all to stand and observe a minute of silence in prayer for the success of this summit conference and in memory of those of our fellow men who, for the love of mankind and of peace, gave up their lives so that we could be free and independent.

On this historic day I am deeply honored and, indeed, very gratified to welcome each and every one of you on behalf of the party, the government and the people of the Republic of Zambia. I am gratified to extend to you all our warmest fraternal greetings and to wish you a most pleasant and enjoyable stay in our young country. Zambians all over the republic feel it a tremendous honor for their country to play host to such an august gathering of distinguished leaders. The Lusaka citizens in particular are proud to be among the first in the world to have in their midst such a large number of world leaders under the same roof.

I know that, as leaders and statesmen, you have tremendous responsibilities in your respective countries. Some of you have come from Addis Ababa, from yet another meeting, while others left their capitals many days ago to be with us on this memorable occasion. Your decision to attend this conference despite your other responsibilities is a source of joy and inspiration to us. We thank you most sincerely for your personal efforts and for the contributions you have made, directly or indirectly, which have made this summit possible.

In welcoming you to our country, we know that the presence of so many leaders in Zambia in this September of 1970 adds a lot to our history. Unfortunately, being young and underdeveloped, we cannot offer adequate facilities. We are very much aware that what we have offered may not meet all your requirements, but I want to assure you that we have provided all that we could afford in the circumstances to make this epoch-making conference possible.

I believe, however, it is appropriate that this conference should be held in Zambia, particularly at the opening of a decade that is likely to be very difficult in many developing countries:

First: We are a young country and only six years old.

Second: We are a developing country.

Third: We are landlocked but still determined to preserve and defend our independence and to further its objectives.

Fourth: Our geographical proximity to countries under colonial rule and oppression by minority regimes has given us special experience in nation-building.

Fifth: Like the nations represented at this conference, we are committed to the principles and ideals of non-alignment as enunciated by the progenitors of this movement. Our offer to host this conference and the erection of Mulungushi Hall and Mulungushi Village are an expression of our dedication to this common cause; a symbol of our commitment to world peace.

September, 1970, is a very important month. Only a few days ago, African leaders were deliberating at the summit of the Organization of African Unity in Addis Ababa. Their declarations form part of the unfolding story of the progress towards unity, economic and social advancement in freedom, peace and justice. Now, in Lusaka, leaders of more than half the world's population are meeting to review the past few years of the non-aligned movement and to discuss, among other things, international problems and prospects for peace and integrative development in the international community. In less than a fortnight, the United Nations General Assembly will be meeting once again in New York; representatives of almost all the people in the world will be discussing the future of mankind. Two factors make the twenty-fifth session of the General Assembly very significant. One is that member nations of the United Nations are this year commemorating the twenty-fifth anniversary of the end of the Second World War and the birth of the United Nations with its Charter for peace, freedom and justice. The other is that this session of the General Assembly will also decide on the designation of the 1970's as the Second United Nations Development Decade—a decision which will bind us for the next ten years.

These momentous events—each with its own objectives —all concern the welfare of man. They underline the fact that the present international situation is unsatisfactory and the urgent need for the establishment of a more decent world order in which men all over the globe can be assured of maximum enjoyment of peace, economic and social progress in freedom and justice regardless of race, religion or station in life.

After a decade that witnessed the growth and intensification of the cold war, the contagious effects of which were felt throughout the world, the Belgrade declaration in 1961 laid the foundation for the policy of non-alignment which was consolidated by the Cairo declaration in 1964. These declarations underlined the urgency for courses of action which were necessary for the achievement of specific objectives, namely,

—the strengthening of the foundations of our independence, freedom and justice;

—the strengthening of the foundations for peace and world security through unity and cooperation among members of the human family;

—the attainment of economic self-reliance among developing countries;

—the total liberation of the areas still under colonial rule and the elimination of imperialism, racial discrimination, oppression and exploitation in whatever shape or form;

—the strengthening of the non-aligned movement and the United Nations.

Non-alignment was a natural and immediate response to the tensions generated by the ideological conflict in the bipolar world. In the heyday of the cold war the need for another independent, impartial but positive voice became necessary and urgent to save the world from the scourge of war. There was a need to assert the voice of many millions of people and nations who did not believe that alliances were inevitable and indispensable for national security, nor that bipolarity was a universal and inevitable law for the establishment of a decent and secure world order.

The reduction of tension and the establishment of a tripolar world have not rendered unnecessary the non-alignment movement. The principles underlying our movement remain valid despite the changes in the immediate circumstances which gave it birth. We still need independence, freedom, justice, peace, balanced economic development and social justice. The urge for non-interference in the internal affairs of other nations, the urge for peaceful co-existence and for the pursuit of independent policies, the eradication of the causes of international tension and the elimination of force in the settlement of international disputes remain fundamental. Furthermore, the danger of weak nations being bullied by the more powerful ones still exists. The hydra of military invasions of one country by another, which characterized international relations before the Second World War, still rears its head in the second half of this century. Nearer home, the minority regimes in rebel Rhodesia, South Africa and the Portuguese colonies in Africa have, with Western support, defied African and world opinion. These regimes continue with their inhuman policies with impunity. Threats of economic strangulation are a political instrument for furthering the aims and objectives of the strong at the expense of the weak nations.

The objectives of non-alignment are intended to give effect to our desire to remain free, independent in peace and justice, to make us less vulnerable to outside pressures and less susceptible to international bullying.

Our non-aligned movement has a very important role to play in the future of not only the developing countries but of the world as a whole. It subsists on a genuine belief among the majority of the people that, in the context of the current international situation, their legitimate interests are not secure and their rights and hopes not possible of realization unless the perilous contradictions which prevail are resolved. The right to participate in the resolution of these contradictions is not a monopoly of the powerful states in the world. Non-aligned countries feel the urge to intensify their search for an international system which guarantees peace and security and provides protection for their independence and maximum freedom to develop their economic and social systems. There is, therefore, nothing irrational about the advocates of non-alignment. The actions of non-aligned countries are natural and justified.

One of the most important characteristics of non-alignment is *unity in diversity*. Many countries represented in this assembly have different economic, social and political systems as well as cultural backgrounds. We respect the differences in our policies. We do not separately or collectively seek to impose our will on any one country. Respect for the independence and sovereignty of other independent nations and non-interference in their internal affairs are fundamental to the future of the non-aligned movement. It is not a national type of unity which we expect to achieve. Geography, history, economic and political factors make this a mere catch-penny dream. What we want and what we shall strive to achieve is a common front to create an atmosphere of independent behavior in international affairs as well as real freedom in our respective countries without outside interference.

Our critics, both in the Western and the Eastern countries, will probably continue to feel that we are pursuing a policy in which the weak countries are able to play off one power against the other. On the contrary, it is not the non-aligned countries who, at the present moment, are playing off one big power against another. Strangely enough, it is the powerful states who are attempting to do this, to divide us and destroy our unity. It is they who assume the right to subvert any nation whom they decide is aligned to the opposing bloc, capitalizing on any differences in the internal political development. But that the policy of non-alignment is appreciated can be seen from the struggle of the aligned to become less aligned, to gain greater freedom of action within the conventional pacts.

The achievements of the first and second conferences of the non-aligned nations have generated new patterns in the international system, the principles of which transcend ideological and military interests. We are part of the changing world. We have a commitment to the world; we are committed to the maintenance of peace and security vital for the unfettered enjoyment of our rights as independent nations.

While the world has succeeded in avoiding a third world war, we have not achieved peace. Major powers have, at best, attained an armed peace for themselves, but they have, unfortunately, been at the root of the violence in the rest of the world. Conflicts in Asia, Latin America and Africa have deprived millions of innocent men, women and children of the much-needed peace for their development.

The crisis in the Middle East has, for a long time, undermined the peace and security in that area. We therefore welcome the cease-fire now in force and the efforts of the United Nations to build a platform for meaningful peace based on justice. We in Zambia stand very firmly by the resolution of the United Nations Security Council of November, 1967, which still provides the best framework for stable peace and relations in that area.

The problems confronting Southeast Asia have continued to exercise our minds. We abhor the dreadful toll in human life which the war in Indochina has brought in its train. We believe that the fate and destiny of the people of Southeast Asia must be decided by the people of the area themselves without outside interference, just as we believe that the future of Europe and of America must be decided by the people of those continents. The complete withdrawal of American troops is, therefore, a prerequisite for any meaningful move towards lasting and genuine peace in Indochina. The continued use of force to impose a socio-political system on other people cannot succeed.

In Latin America, thanks to the wisdom and statesmanship of the leaders, tremendous efforts have been made fairly successfully to have such crises as arose resolved around the conference table rather than on the battlefield. It is my sincere hope that the solution to problems among Latin American brothers will help guarantee peace so that people of that continent can enjoy the benefits of economic development and improved social welfare.

The turbulent events in the first decade of African independence have shaken many countries. For a time a dark shadow of doubt had been cast over the future of the continent. However, I hope that the 1970's will see a complete return to stability and confidence which, in turn, should provide an atmosphere conducive to economic and social development.

In southern Africa in particular, imperialism, colonialism and racial oppression and exploitation still reign. The indifference of major powers and the overt political, economic and military support given by the Western nations to the regimes in South Africa, Portugal and rebel Rhodesia have given a stamp of recognition and encouragement to the dominance exercised by the minorities over the majorities. In the new situation, South Africa has strengthened her hold over the indigenous majority; the Vorster regime is able to extend its tentacles of political, economic and military power and influence in support of colonial minority regimes in Angola, Mozambique and rebel Rhodesia. The Portuguese position in Guinea Bissau has also been strengthened.

In recent years, the Western countries have added a new element to their indifference over issues concerning southern Africa. The growth of their investment in and the sale of arms to South Africa have strengthened the hand of apartheid and enabled it to extend the boundaries of its influence. South Africa has defied the United Nations over the illegal presence of her security forces in Rhodesia. Britain, on the other hand, has not even protested about this illegal act. South Africa has further defied world opinion and the United Nations over her continued illegal administration of Namibia. There are, indeed, countries who today appear prepared to support South Africa's case on this matter in order to preserve their own selfish interests. The South African influence in Angola and Mozambique has complicated the process of decolonization in those areas. Some member states of the United Nations would, we know, prefer to ignore this fact. They find greater security for their interests in the *status quo* than in change which conforms to the Charter of the United Nations.

We in Zambia, have pointed out the dangers of strengthening the military position of South Africa:

First: Apartheid is, as we know, a diabolical system which gives political, economic and military power exclusively to a racist regime. At present, three million white people have taken over control of eighty-seven per cent of the land, leaving only thirteen per cent for the majority—almost fourteen million—to depend on for their livelihood. South Africa's propaganda would have us believe that the thirteen per cent allocated to the African people is the most fertile land in that country.

Second: The object of the Bantustans is not to build nation-states in South Africa, but to establish a system under which ethnic conflicts can be provoked if necessary, and the foundation for unity among African people completely destroyed. A system which concentrates black populations in specific areas also makes South Africa's military operations against the majority of the people more practical and effective without risking loss of life among the whites.

Third: Namibia will be more difficult for the United Nations to take over and administer as South Africa's newly acquired military strength is geared to the defense of her illegal presence in that area.

Fourth: South Africa's commitment in Angola, Mozambique and rebel Rhodesia grows daily with her capability to extend military support to those areas. The object of South Africa's military involvement is to protect her economic and financial interests and to give effect to her political intentions.

Fifth: South Africa is committed not only to the expansion of the so-called "area of co-prosperity" but also to the extension of her influence in independent countries north of the Zambezi. Her objective is to undermine the liberation movement and the independence of African countries.

The negative response of the major Western countries over the question of South Africa, Rhodesia and the Portuguese position in Africa has greatly contributed to the crisis which is developing in this region. They have the capacity to help bring about peaceful changes and the realization of self-determination for the majority of the people. Their refusal to participate in effective actions designed to end colonial and racial domination in southern Africa and in Guinea Bissau is responsible for the expanding commitment of South Africa in the area, for the arms race in Africa and for the dangers inherent in the escalation of the conflict. Those are people who say they are civilized, and they get support for a regime like that. This is why the continued sale of arms to South Africa and Portugal is the greatest blunder the major Western countries have made over this question.

We welcome the decision of the Organization for African Unity to send a delegation to the countries now selling arms or intending to sell arms to South Africa. I hope Western countries can heed our warning that those who delay the discharge of justice, those who stand in the way of peaceful change towards majority rule, make violence inevitable.

The strengthening of the United Nations is one of the fundamental objectives of non-aligned countries. However, as long as this world body is not universal in terms of representation, our efforts will not be very effective. The exclusion of the People's Republic of China, representing almost one-third of the world's population, is a blunder and there can be no legitimate reason for refusing her admission to the world body—none whatsoever.

There is also the question of divided states which, since Cairo, has continued to be a source of misunderstanding. Not much progress has been made over the question of Korea, Vietnam and Germany. At the root of the failure to resolve the problem of divided states is the involvement of great powers.

Finally, another phenomenon of the period after the second conference of non-aligned countries is the growing gap between the rich and the poor, between the developed and developing nations, between the continents in the north and those in the south of this world. The existence of the gap between the rich and the poor nations breeds exploitation of the economically weak by the strong. The UNCTAD Conferences held in Geneva and New Delhi, as well as the First United Nations Development Decade, have failed to achieve their objectives.

These then are some of the basic problems which have bedeviled international relations since the last summit of the non-aligned countries in Cairo.

The United Nations machinery has been thrown into a state of virtual inertia by the failure of member states to implement the hundreds of decisions and resolutions passed by the General Assembly, the Security Council, other agencies and international organizations. This, and the indifference of great powers in particular, have undermined the authority of the United Nations considerably.

This is, indeed, a challenging period and the task of the non-aligned governments is tremendous. The leaders gathered in this hall must, in the next few days, consider seriously specific measures to give effect to the tenets of the non-aligned movement, the Charter of the United Nations and the fundamental principles upon which our respective nations are built.

Non-alignment as a policy implies a course or courses of action designed to achieve *inter alia* the objectives I referred to earlier in my statement. Individually, we cannot hope to influence the course of events towards peace; but collectively in our non-alignment movement with its commitment to peace and justice we can generate tremendous political and moral force in international relations for the benefit of mankind.

For some developing countries this decade is likely to be a trying one. The internal reorganization of our social and economic systems is an imperative necessity. The effects of such change will bear very heavily on political developments. Yet, if we are to succeed in defending our independence we have no choice but to take control of and improve the instruments for national reconstruction—economic, social and military—together with other elements of national strength. Economic self-reliance supported by the acquisition of sufficient technical know-how is a *sine qua non* of a successful national development effort. The developing countries, as a group of nations committed to a common cause and collective action, have a primary responsibility for their own development and defense. Developed countries may help, but the developing nations, in the final analysis, have to shoulder the responsibility for their success or failure.

In considering collective measures we have to take to achieve our objectives, let us reaffirm our faith in non-alignment. We cannot hope to succeed in strengthening the United Nations if we are already divided by military and political pacts. We must reaffirm our faith in the United Nations Charter and urge all member states to observe strictly its provisions as the first and vital step towards the realization of its aims.

But much more is required than mere reaffirmation and pledges. We must move non-alignment out of what critics consider mere political and idle rhetoric. We must work out and agree on common action to give substance to the movement not only in the political field, but in economic and technical fields which will add to our unity and strength. Let us, therefore, seek areas of meaningful collective action; let us increase our capacity for creating a better environment, a better tomorrow for development in peace, freedom and justice.

A call for action is not enough unless there exists an adequate machinery to carry it out. Perhaps this is the one factor to which not much attention was given in the past. We agree we need *peace* and that *peace* is the theme of the non-aligned movement, but it is quite clear that peace can only be secured and maintained successfully if it is based on meaningful and sound economic development and social justice. It is my submission that the time has come for the non-aligned countries to take measures in this direction.

Furthermore, it is essential for non-aligned and developing countries to seek an effective strategy for their own development. This strategy must be centered around economic, financial and technical cooperation. We may not have enough to go around. We need not have enough to start this important initiative. The intention is not to replace altogether the help from and cooperation with developed countries. They are, after all, part and parcel of the growing international community. Our poverty affects them just as they benefit from our economic strength. Our main goal in the common strategy must be to reduce our dependence on those powerful nations who, for their own interests, expect political and ideological support in return for economic, financial and technical assistance.

We do not seek to dictate changes in the pattern of international relations. What we seek is unity through economic and technical cooperation to prevent the stronger nations from imposing their will on us separately or collectively. We seek a place of honor and respect in the world. This, I submit, is not an unreasonable demand; it is natural and fundamental to a people engaged in a genuine search for a better world order. It is, therefore, essential that the leaders of the non-aligned world examine the existing potential for cooperation within their regions. Trade among non-aligned countries is almost insignificant. Economic and technical cooperation exists mostly between the developed and developing countries. The extension of economic, financial and technical cooperation is essential to the success of non-alignment; it will bring about better understanding among us and also help accelerate economic growth.

Since localized conflicts are likely to continue in the developing countries, we clearly will be the victims of stagnation, destruction and hardship arising out of the violence which may occur. Only we can avoid our being made victims of the local conflicts. Only we can bring about peace and stability in our regions through effective action. We need economic strength to make our countries less vulnerable to the powerful pressures from outside.

It is for this reason that we genuinely need the machinery

for maintaining contact among us to ensure continuity in the development of the non-aligned movement and the implementation of our decisions.

The pursuit of our objectives and the call for collective action should not be a source of concern to any nation not represented in this assembly. We have no large armies; nor is common defense in our program of action. We threaten no power and have nothing against the powerful states. All we want is to make sure that our political freedom and economic and social progress are secure in our hands and are not subject to manipulation to benefit other nations against our interests. That is all we seek.

There is strength in unity; there is even greater strength in unity of action in the pursuit of our common purpose.

In conclusion let me emphasize that this assembly of world leaders is, in itself, an important factor and adds to the landmarks of the history of non-alignment. But it also represents a challenge, for while our presence together is memorable, the decisions which we are expected to make are of greater importance and significance for the future of mankind. We must proceed with courage and determination. I have no doubt that, in the next few days, you will bring your wisdom and eminence to bear on world problems, on peace, freedom, development and international cooperation. May the decisions made in this Mulungushi Hall be for the benefit of mankind as a whole.

As I declare this conference open, the peoples of the non-aligned countries and many men of goodwill the world over, and particularly Zambians who are deeply honored by your presence here, would want me, on their behalf, to wish this third summit conference of non-aligned countries every success.

ADDRESS BY
PRESIDENT JOSIP BROZ TITO
OF YUGOSLAVIA

With your permission, I should like, on behalf of the peoples of Yugoslavia, to address this distinguished gathering, attended by such an impressive number of statesmen, representing about one-third of mankind and one-half of all the world's countries.

First of all, in the name of the government of my country and the Yugoslav delegation, and on my own personal behalf, may I extend heartfelt gratitude to the hosts of this historic meeting, the people and government of Zambia, and particularly His Excellency, President Kaunda, for their cordial hospitality. At the same time, I should like to tender recognition to the great efforts they have invested in order to assure the best possible working conditions for the Third Conference of the Heads of State and Government of Non-Aligned Countries in this lovely city of Lusaka.

May I also take this opportunity to express appreciation to the foreign ministers of non-aligned countries who have done so much work in Dar-es-Salaam and recently in Lusaka to prepare for this conference.

It was, I think, an extremely felicitous decision to hold the third conference of non-aligned countries here, in this part of liberated Africa, in the vicinity of which brutal colonial suppression still continues. For, the great majority of the population in neighboring territories, oppressed by racialist lawlessness and tyranny, rightfully expects not only the non-aligned countries but also the United Nations—especially this year when the world organization celebrates its twenty-fifth anniversary—to take a decisive step towards the definitive abolition of colonial servitude and the emancipation of peoples.

The situation in southern Africa today is alarming in the extreme and makes it necessary not only for the non-aligned countries, but the entire democratic and peace-minded public of the world, to take a determined stand. This is all the more true in view of the outright manifestation of aggressive and expansionist tendencies towards the newly liberated African countries. To make matters worse, these tendencies are being supported by certain reactionary circles in the world who endeavor to terminate the international isolation of racialist regimes in these territories and to consolidate footholds of imperialist policy there.

I stress this at the very outset because I feel that support for the peoples now fighting, under the most difficult conceivable conditions, for their liberation from colonial suppression—the most glaring disgrace of the twentieth century —is a question that should be accorded priority also by this eminent gathering. But our support for those peoples should not be declarative alone; we should not let matters rest at appeals and resolutions. We who have come together here must agree not only to extend moral and political support but also the most effective possible material assistance to those who are fighting with arms in hand against colonial oppression and racial discrimination. We must also reach agreement to undertake an effective action against all those who sabotage the adopted decisions of the United Nations relevant to the urgent and definitive liquidation of the remnants of colonialism. For we cannot reconcile ourselves with the fact that colonial and racialist regimes are being tolerated more than two decades after the adoption of the Charter of the United Nations and the Declaration of Human Rights, as well as a full decade after the adoption of the declaration on the final liquidation of colonialism. It is my profound conviction that this distinguished gathering will display unanimity on these questions. And that would be a guarantee that the spirit of unity and action will also be transferred to the United Nations, particularly to the forthcoming twenty-fifth anniversary session.

During the past decade, the policy of non-alignment asserted itself powerfully in international affairs, for it showed the way out of the troubled cold war period when mankind tottered on the brink of a catastrophe. It opened up new prospects for international relations which had been staggering under the burden of a sharp bloc confrontation. It stressed the principles of independence, autonomous development of countries and comprehensive international cooperation on the basis of equality, as well as the need for the accelerated advancement of the developing countries. It threw light on the contradictions of the contemporary world and the causes of instability in international relations, while bending its efforts toward their removal. It demanded that crucial international problems be solved by peaceful means.

The appeal sent out by the Belgrade conference to the big powers to establish contact with each other and to solve, by negotiation, and not by the use of force, the controversial problems that had emerged as the legacy of the Second World War was not without its repercussions. The declaration adopted then was acclaimed by all peace-minded people throughout the world. It met with the approval of all those who considered its principles, and the spirit imbuing it, as the sole alternative to the danger of war, and as the road toward the creation of better and more equitable relations among states and peoples.

At the Cairo conference, the principles of peaceful and active co-existence among states, irrespective of differences in ideology and social system—and these are the salient features of non-aligned policy—were powerfully affirmed once again. These principles, as a lasting value of non-alignment, have been confirmed in all critical situations during the past twenty-year period in international relations. With increasing power, they are working against domination and the use of force, against interference in the internal affairs of other peoples. In a word, the positive effect of non-aligned policy on international events is now an indisputable reality.

True, it encounters strong resistance on the part of those forces that are endeavoring in various ways to turn back the clock of history. These are the protagonists of force and domination who do not, naturally, find the anti-imperialist character of non-aligned policy to their liking. But, whether they like it or not, mankind, in its vast majority, has accepted that policy as the only possible way to set the world on a new and democratic track.

The policy of force, aggression, intervention and interference into the affairs of other countries is still constantly present in international relations. It represents a danger, not only for the non-aligned, but also for all those countries which are guided by the principles of equal international cooperation in their foreign political orientation and which do not want their sovereignty, security and progress to depend on the disposition and goodwill of whatever foreign power.

We, who advocate the respect of the principles of international behavior contained in the United Nations Charter, must jointly resist all manifestations of force and all forms of domination, show a greater degree of solidarity and act jointly. Especially when it is necessary to give support and assistance to those non-aligned and other countries and peoples which, as the victims of aggression, find themselves in a difficult situation.

Such policy of force and foreign intervention comes to expression in its most flagrant form in Indochina and the Near East today. The heroic struggle of the Vietnamese peo-

ple for freedom and independence, to which the non-aligned
countries are giving powerful support, must, to the interest
of peace and the implementation of the principles for which
we are striving, lead to the ending of war and the ensurance
of the legitimate rights of the people of Vietnam freely to
decide on its fate as soon as possible.

The policy of force and intervention has recently come
to expression in Cambodia, a non-aligned and peace-loving
and until yesterday flourishing country which has, today,
together with Vietnam, become an arena of destruction and
all horrors which war brings with it.

Cambodia, led by Prince Sihanouk, has for years successfully defended her independence and sovereignty and,
understandably, has been trying to remain outside conflicts
in this part of the world. However, under outside pressure
and influence, changes have taken place in this country,
contrary to the will of her people, which is therefore giving
unanimous resistance not only to foreign interventionists, but
also to domestic collaborators.

This is why Yugoslavia has at the very beginning condemned the *coup d'état* and outside intervention as an attack
on the independence, neutrality and non-aligned policy of
Cambodia, considering legal only the government formed by
the head of state, Prince Sihanouk, the government which
is presently continuing the policy of defending national independence and non-alignment in far more difficult conditions.

We are convinced—and this is proved by the experience
from the past—that peace in Southeast Asia can be established
only through the strict respect and realization of the rights of
the peoples of Vietnam, Cambodia and other peoples of
this region to freedom and self-determination, without outside
interference.

The key precondition for this, in our opinion, is the
urgent, unconditioned and complete withdrawal of American
troops and their allies from Vietnam and other countries of

Indochina, so as to enable the peoples of this region to decide on their fate themselves, without any interference from outside.

It is our belief that, today, the adoption of the policy of non-alignment by peoples living in Southeast Asia as an authentic expression of their most profound desire for independence and their own roads of development will greatly contribute to this. For this reason, we welcome with special satisfaction the presence at and participation of representatives of the Provisional Revolutionary Government of the Republic of South Vietnam in the present gathering. This presence is both logical and understandable since the foreign political orientation of the provisional government and the basic aims of the heroic struggle of the Vietnamese people coincide in their essence with the aspirations of the non-aligned countries to live in peace and freedom, without foreign pressures and interventions.

The inclusion of representatives of the provisional revolutionary government into the work of the conference of the highest-ranking representatives of the non-aligned countries is very significant, both for the movement of the non-aligned in general—since we are proving in deed the consistent adherence to the principle of unreserved support to peoples struggling against foreign intervention—and, as we believe, the provisional revolutionary government itself. Included into the movement of the non-aligned with support we can give to it, it is strengthening its independent position in international relations. Finally, it is significant for the prospects of peace in this part of the world.

The same has been the case with our attitude towards Israeli aggression against the United Arab Republic and other Arab countries. Why has Yugoslavia, from the very first day, given all possible support to these countries? Because it has been clear since the very beginning that what is in question is aggression with far-reaching imperialist aims. Anyway, this has been proved by Israel's later behavior which has not accepted the Security Council resolution and which, in different ways, has been preventing the peaceful solving of this crisis. Developments have shown that Israel's existence has not been brought into question and that aggression on the Arab countries has not been motivated by defense but by conquering aspirations. We have positively assessed the fact that Israel has accepted Rogers's proposal for talks on the peaceful solving of the conflict with the Arab countries. As we can see, however, it has quickly been proved that this has been merely a maneuver, for Israel has interrupted the talks before they have actually started. This is completely the style of Israel's behavior since 1948 onwards.

We cannot and must not remain indifferent towards such a state of affairs. For, if all the problems of this region fail to be radically solved this time, too—which above all presumes the withdrawal of Israeli troops from all the invaded Arab territories and the exercise of the legitimate rights of the people of Palestine, i.e. the ensurance of its right to existence —we shall be faced with new dangers which may have far-reaching consequences on world peace.

All these matters have constantly been the focus of our attention. Naturally, too, they cause us a great deal of anxiety, not only as regards the fate of the peoples threatened by imperialist aggression, but also the international community in its entirety, unless it finds the strength to remove the causes of such manifestations. If we permit the idea of "might makes right" to entrench itself, all of us stand in danger and, at one time or another, every non-aligned and any other independent country could become the victim of aggression. Therefore, in all such cases, we must act in unity and offer resistance.

Support and assistance for the victims of aggression are indispensable, not only as a reflection of solidarity and friendship, but also to safeguard the vital national interests of each country, and particularly of the non-aligned. Open and uncompromising opposition to force and aggression; common resistance to pressure, to all attempts to meddle in the internal affairs of others, to interventions and to imposing the will of one upon another—are, as we see it, an imperative of the times and the essence of non-alignment under present international conditions.

Undoubtedly, then, there are many things in today's world to give us cause for serious concern. But some signs hold out hope that crucial problems can be solved, given goodwill and the readiness to settle them peaceably. This is also demonstrated by the most recent processes in Europe where regulation and stabilization of conditions have been inaugurated. For many years, Europe was a region rent by the aftermath of the war, tension, cold war and confrontation, with far-reaching negative consequences for the entire world. Even today, problems in Europe are no less complicated than they are in other parts of the world. However, when mutual contacts and talks were initiated, particularly of late, the first concrete results were quick to be achieved. This is also reflected in the recently concluded treaty between the Soviet Union and the Federal German Republic on non-recourse to force in mutual relations.

We attach great significance to present positive processes in Europe not only for relaxation on this continent but for their positive influence on the world situation generally. For they can be highly instrumental in facilitating the solution of unsettled international problems to which I have referred.

One of the major problems we confront, one of the long-term preoccupations of the non-aligned countries, is undoubtedly the present state of world economic relations. The fact is that we are still far from any tangible results in terms of achieving a more harmonious economic development throughout the world as a whole, which would assume narrowing the gap between the developed and developing countries. The uneven rhythm of development continues to widen this gap, to undermine general stability in the world and pave the way for technological colonialism which in the ultimate analysis offers former metropolises and certain other countries an opportunity for political pressure and influence. It would therefore be necessary for non-aligned policy, to a much greater extent than has hitherto been the case, to occupy itself with problems of development in the broadest sense of the term.

It is indispensable, in the first place, for the developing countries to rely above all on their own forces and to develop and utilize to the maximum all their internal human and material potential. Further, it will be necessary to promote mutual cooperation among developing countries more intensively and to exploit all the advantages offered by economic integration and cooperation. But the differences in the degree of economic development are so great that these efforts cannot succeed in their purpose without comprehensive international cooperation and genuine, lasting assistance from the broader international community. Unfortunately, I must note that this indispensable support has been far below requirements and realistic potentialities. The reason for this does not lie in a lack of material possibilities on the part of the developed countries; what is involved are political and selfish motives and the absence of readiness to solve this world-wide problem. Also, the desire to exploit economic superiority as a means of pressure for the achievement of political goals and to maintain relations of domination and inequality. It is interesting that certain smaller countries, and even less developed ones, have demonstrated far more understanding and willingness to extend such support than the biggest and richest of the world's countries.

Over two hundred billion dollars were expended on armaments last year. Only ten per cent of this sum would suffice under present conditions to meet the needs of the developing countries for foreign financial resources. In any case, a decisive change is needed in international economic relations and cooperation, particularly in terms of the policies of the developed countries. It is imperative for those countries to accept the new policy of development and to help in its achievement. The forthcoming development decade should be a precise and concrete program, and not an empty declaration.

The United Nations, with its progressive objectives and principles, inscribed in the Charter, is undoubtedly one of the most significant achievements of our civilization. The United Nations has helped the ideals of freedom and independence attain a high degree of affirmation. At certain critical points, the world organization has risen to meet the challenge of its task: it has helped surmount the immediate danger of a widespread war. But it also reflects the problems, difficulties and contradictions of contemporary international relations. However, the United Nations, despite this, remains an irreplaceable and indispensable instrument of international cooperation. One of the essential conditions for its efficacy is the adaptation of its work to present-day requirements and conditions, and the achievement of full universality. I am referring, above all, to the restoration of the legitimate rights of the People's Republic of China, and the admission of other countries which are not yet members of the world organization. It is high time the world organization adopted the declaration on the codification of the principles of peaceful and active co-existence.

The twenty-fifth anniversary session of the General Assembly and our conference are linked both in time and substance: For us, the non-aligned countries, these two events represent a whole, invested—one might say—with the same historic meaning. The reaffirmation of the principles of the Charter and the strengthening of the United Nations—these are, among others, the objectives towards which our gathering also strives.

I therefore feel that the twenty-fifth session of the United Nations should truly be a historic one, not in terms of declarations but concrete decisions. This session should initiate solutions of problems which could not be solved in the past owing to the resistance of forces opposing the democratization of international relations and equality between the small and the large.

In speaking of the democratization of international relations, there is no need to stress that this is a contemporary requirement. It must bring about the full participation of all factors in world affairs, render it impossible to apply the policy of force, liquidate imperialist and colonialist suppression and all kinds of hegemony. The world in which we live must be developed by all of us and each one must be in the position to shoulder his part of the rights and responsibilities. Otherwise, the world will continue to be hopelessly divided into the all-powerful and the disenfranchised, the rich and the poor, the privileged and the discriminated.

The attempts to solve international problems by piece-meal methods, by individual arrangements between the big powers or military-political blocs, may lead to temporary and perhaps even useful solutions. We have never opposed the dialogue between the big powers—and in any case the non-aligned countries called for it at the Belgrade conference —as they bear a greater responsibility for preserving world peace. But we are against the monopoly of the big powers, against any division into spheres of interests and against any dialogue among them which would work to the detriment of third countries.

We are aware that the development of new democratic international relations requires not only considerable effort and perseverance but also a great deal of time. But every step, no matter how modest, towards genuine equality, democratization and general prosperity is a contribution to the world's progressive transformation.

We have gathered here to assess the present moment in world history. This moment holds out the hope and promise of a fairer, more peaceful world, but simultaneously harbors many dangers to the existence of mankind and civilization. The times we live in open up great vistas for universal progress. But many responsible factors in the world lack the readiness and will to set out with determination on the road to lasting peace and progress and to subordinate all narrow interests to the vital needs of mankind.

The vision of a new type of international relations assumes lasting and universal peace, an effective system of collective security, general and complete disarmament, transcendence of the gap between developed and developing, and above all co-existence among peoples and countries regardless of their size and political system.

In this divided world, in the period of strong trends toward alignment with military-political groupings, it was not an easy matter to embark on this common road of ours and to stand firm on the positions of non-alignment. But we have remained staunch as it has been our conviction that this is the most constructive way we can contribute to the peace and progress of mankind.

The very fact that almost three times as many countries are attending this conference as participated in the first one is the best confirmation that our policies are correct. Today, we enjoy the sincere and widespread support of the democratic and progressive public of the world, which encourages us in our efforts to achieve our goals. We are also mindful of the fact that in the present-day world, which grows increasingly interdependent and in which equality is an imperative, any monopoly is untenable. We therefore consider alien to us the thought of exclusiveness of any kind, any special rights or any persuasion that useful proposals and actions originate only with us. Our platform presupposes the broadest possible cooperation, always and with everyone, wherever it consolidates peace, promotes equality and helps remove all forms of subordination.

We have often heard the objection raised that we wish

to form a new bloc. Not only do we not want to do so, but we are working for the transcendence and disappearance of the existing blocs.

Similarly, remarks are frequently heard to the effect that non-alignment is characterized by passiveness and maneuvering between the blocs. We are, however, highly committed and have put forward our own programs which in no way signify reconciliation to the present state of the world but rather a concrete contribution toward changing it for the better.

We are further criticized as being against the big powers. We are not against the big powers, we are only against power politics.

It is said that the non-aligned can wield no influence because they have no weapons or wealth. It is for this precise reason that we are striving for a world in which arms and riches will not be the decisive basis for power and influence.

When we strive for a more balanced world development, we do not do so only for the purpose of assisting the less developed, but also because it is an economic necessity in the interests of all.

We are not, therefore, fighting only for a better place for ourselves in this world, we are fighting for a better world generally. United by these aspirations, we must also unite our possibilities, multiply mutual ties and expand the area of our cooperation. Solidarity in matters of preserving independence and consolidating security is the basis of our close relations and a precondition for our ability to continue acting together.

It would therefore be indispensable for us to develop such a system of cooperation and relations as would assure effective mutual assistance and solidarity.

The non-aligned countries must assert themselves still further as an active factor in international relations. If they join efforts and act in unity on the international scene, they can accomplish a great deal. It does not suffice for them to be the conscience of mankind; they must rather be a force contributing actively to the creation of a better morrow.

In conclusion, I assure you that Yugoslavia will continue in the future, as she has in the past, to strive sincerely and consistently for the achievement of the positions and conclusions we adopt here together.

ADDRESS BY
PRIME MINISTER INDIRA GANDHI
OF INDIA

I welcome this opportunity to give the greetings of the people of India to the government and people of Zambia and to the heads and representatives of the nations who have gathered here. We must also thank President Tito. But for his efforts this meeting would not have taken place. We are glad that this non-aligned conference is meeting for the first time in southern Africa, close to the spirit, the mood and the very heartbeat of Africa.

Here in Lusaka, we can feel the ebb and flow of the continuing battle against remnants of colonialism in Angola and Mozambique. We can feel the vibrations of the struggle against the minority government in Zimbabwe, against the apartheid policies of the racist regime in the Union of South Africa and the national movements in Namibia and in Guinea Bissau. These freedom fighters are engaged in the same battle as we were only recently. They are risking their lives for the same principles that we hold dear. All of us who are meeting here extend our support to these brave men and women.

As I said yesterday, the revolution of our times is unfinished, and the purpose of this conference is to formulate a clear program of action to carry it forward. This is the challenge that the decade of the seventies places before the non-aligned countries.

Only a short while ago, the issues of war and peace, of the disposal of human beings and their destinies, were decided in a few capitals of the world. No longer is it so.

Because millions of people in the resurgent continents of Asia, of Africa, of Latin America and the Caribbean have come into their own. Because we determined that decisions involving us—whether concerning war and peace or the direction and pace of our social, economic and political development—could be made only by us, in our own way, and in our own countries. That is how non-alignment was born. It expressed our individual and collective sovereignty, our devotion to freedom and peace and our urgent need to give a better life to our people and the opportunity to live in freedom, in dignity and in peace. At no time was there any intention to set up a third world.

This is our endeavor. The odds are tremendous. Each step has met with criticism and opposition. But we have carried on. Let us not be deterred by cynics and the hostile propaganda of the powerful media of communications. From the beginning, there has been no lack of inquisitors who looked upon non-alignment as heresy, and distorted its meaning. They said it would not work. And yet, can we not answer back today in the famous words of Galileo—"And yet, it moves!"

The criticism of non-alignment has shifted on two counts. Those who now concede that non-alignment had some utility in the days of the cold war confrontation maintain that this is no longer so. The reviling is not any more about the basis and principle, but of its practice.

Have the non-aligned states lost their relevance? The answer is an emphatic no. Twenty-five years after the last holocaust, the world is not yet on the brink of peace. The nuclear balance of terror still confronts us. The war in Vietnam is said to be waged with "conventional" weapons, yet these include chemical contamination of food and plant life. The only way to have a clean war is not to have a war at all. Hence India stands and works for total disarmament.

The great powers certainly have the major responsibility for international peace and security. We welcome all initiatives towards the resolution of differences through negotiations, but even if they reach accord on their common interests and decide upon mutually acceptable limitation of strategic arsenals, the rest of the world, of which we form a considerable part, could hardly remain mere onlookers. We have an equal stake in peace, but the quality of this peace should be such as will ensure our own sovereignty and security.

Not only national honor but national interest demand that we do not mortgage our decisions in domestic and in international affairs to any foreign dictate. This was one element of our policy of non-alignment. As the logical corollary, we rejected the enmities of our erstwhile rulers. We cultivated relations with all countries. As my father declared: "We are in no camp and in no military alliance. The only camp we should like to be in is the camp of peace which should include as many countries as possible."

I am grateful to this conference for the gracious gesture in memory of my father and to the many distinguished delegates who made references to him.

We decided that our respective territories should not be used for the subjugation of other people, for subversion or for the carving out of spheres of influence. Indian manpower and resources had been used for imperialist purposes. Once free, we declared that this would no longer be permitted.

Subjected to domination, exploitation and the humiliation of racial discrimination as we all had been, how could we compromise with racialism in any form? The pernicious theory that one man is superior to another merely on the ground of race or birth has been proved to be false, yet it continues to dominate the thinking of many.

We believe that today's world is a single entity. We are deeply convinced that by staying out of military pacts the non-aligned countries can use their collective wisdom and influence to tip the balance of power in favor of peace and international cooperation.

These have been the positive achievements of non-alignment. If today there is a weakening of the belief in the efficacy of military pacts, if historic animosities are giving way to essays in friendship and cooperation, if a breath of realism is influencing international policies towards detente, the nations assembled here can claim some credit. However, this should not lull us into complacency, but encourage us to persevere.

The big powers have never accepted the validity of non-alignment. Neither colonialism nor racialism have vanished. The old comes back in new guise. There are subtle intrigues to undermine our self-confidence and to sow dissensions and mutual distrust among us. Powerful vested interests, domestic and foreign, are combining to erect new structures of neo-colonialism. These dangers can be combated by our being united in our adherence to the basic tenets of non-alignment.

I have touched upon certain general points but, on such an occasion, one cannot ignore some of the explosive situations which confront the world.

I should like to take this opportunity to convey our admiration and best wishes to President Gamal Abdel Nasser for his statesmanship and courage in accepting the cease-fire. We disapprove of Israel's intransigence. Israel should be prevailed upon to comply fully with the United Nations Security Council resolution of November, 1967. We cannot ignore the inalienable right of the people of Palestine to the homelands from which they were exiled.

The situation in Southeast Asia has further deteriorated. We are deeply concerned about the spreading of the conflict to Cambodia. All foreign forces should withdraw from the various countries of Indochina, the lead being given by the United States. Our assessment, based on talks with the various parties concerned, has led us to believe that a broad-based government, comprising all elements of South Vietnam, would pave the way for the success of the Paris talks. Recent developments in Laos indicate the possibility of talks between the two sides there. As a member and chairman of the International Commission, we have offered our good offices to both the concerned parties for this purpose. To preserve peace and to provide for the reconstruction of this war-torn area, some kind of international convention or agreement should be signed by all the parties concerned as well as the great powers and other interested parties to ensure respect for the neutrality, independence, territorial integrity and sovereignty of all the Indochina states.

We have been deeply disturbed by the reported intention of the United Kingdom and other governments to supply arms to the government of South Africa. This dangerous and retrograde step will threaten the neighbors of South Africa and also the Indian Ocean area. Any accretion to South Africa's military capability will abet its policy of apartheid and racial discrimination, and may encourage it to annex other territories. The argument that this is being done to protect the so-called security of sea routes is untenable. We would like the Indian Ocean to be an area of peace and cooperation. Military bases of outside powers will create tension and great power rivalry.

The spirit of freedom goes hand in hand with the spirit of equality. Beyond the political problems of the unfinished revolution, there are complex and difficult economic tasks. However, a realistic appraisal of our natural resources, our capacities and our competence reveals the possibility for us to work together to reduce our dependence on those who do not respect our sovereignty so that economic leverage for thinly disguised political purposes cannot be used against us. Neo-colonialism has no sympathy with our efforts to achieve self-reliance. It seeks to perpetuate our position of disadvantage. International markets are so manipulated in such a way that primary producing countries have a permanent handicap. The levers of technology are also operated against us through unequal collaboration and royalty agreements.

Hence we have to redouble our effort to gain for each

nation the opportunity to develop to its full stature. The primary responsibility rests upon each developing country. But we also owe a duty to one another. The fallacy that there is no complementarity between our economies has so far made it difficult to realize the undoubted potential of mutual cooperation. There is greater complementarity among our economies than between the economies of developed nations. Yet advanced nations have been more successful in forging instruments of cooperation among themselves and our own effort in this direction has not even begun. The potential of trade and economic cooperation among us has been left virtually unexplored. By meeting each other's needs, we would diversify our trade, safeguard it against the caprices of international commerce and reduce our dependence on middlemen and brokers.

This conference should formulate the manner in which we could strengthen one another, and give due priority in our national policies to positive measures for mutual cooperation. Such cooperation will help each of us to find some solutions to our respective problems and also give us the capability to induce these changes in the economic system at the global level.

Through the United Nations Conference on Trade and Development, we have tried to persuade the international community to make the changes which have been overdue in the economic system. This is now well understood all over the world. Yet only some have been accepted in principle and even their implementation has been tardy. In a few weeks the second development decade will be launched by the United Nations General Assembly. So far there has been little progress in evolving the guidelines for international cooperation. Many nations which have the capacity, and if I may say so, the duty to make a decisive contribution, hedge their statements with reservation. For too long has international cooperation been viewed as a one-way traffic from the rich to the poor nations.

As the Prime Minister of Guyana said yesterday, between ourselves we possess the major part of the world's natural resources. Our manpower resources are no less plentiful. It should not be beyond our ingenuity to develop these resources and employ the manpower for the production of wealth for our peoples. Because of historical circumstances, economic relations have not been developed among ourselves, but between each of our countries and the erstwhile metropolitan powers. We can now make the first attempts to discover areas of cooperation in many fields of development, generation of power, development of agriculture, improvement of roadways, railways and telecommunications, the expansion of higher education and training in science and technology. If we decide—and I hope we shall—to make a beginning with this study, India will be glad to play its modest part.

We all recognize the malaise afflicting the development process. We know of the growing gap between developed and developing countries, between the northern and southern hemispheres, of the indifference of the affluent, the disappointments of the first development decade, the failure of the affluent countries to transfer even one per cent of their gross national product. We are painfully familiar with the pitfalls of "aid," in which the bulk of credits are tied to purchases from donor countries and with the fact that a big portion of new credits goes to the repayment of old loans. But the question is: Must we endlessly wait in the hope that some day the developed countries will undergo a change of heart and realize that disparities in the world are not in their own interest? I am not a pessimist, but I think we should not expect miracles of magnanimity. Even if this should happen I am afraid that it would be of no avail in the absence of the right conditions in our countries. We must determine to help ourselves, to sacrifice, to pool our resources of knowledge and initiative. We must work together on a bilateral, regional and multilateral basis.

From my own experience, I know that will-power, consistent endeavor and the capacity for sacrifice sustained and strengthened us during our struggle for political independence. These same qualities will help us towards economic freedom.

The power to question is the basis of all human progress. We are free because we question the right of others to rule over us. But intellectual and cultural emancipation is just beginning. We are rediscovering ourselves and the fact that a country sees things in terms of its own geography and history. Those who dominated the world's political affairs and manned its economic controls also imposed a monopoly of ideas. For years we accepted their values, their image of the world and strangely enough even of ourselves. Whether we like it or not, we have been pushed into postures of imitation. We have now to break away from borrowed models of development and evolve models of the worthwhile life which are more relevant to our conditions—not necessarily as a group but as individual countries with their distinctive personalities.

The world today is united in peril, not merely the peril from nuclear destruction but the more insidious daily pollution of our environment. It should be united in prosperity and in the blossoming of the spirit of man. The non-aligned countries must be in the vanguard of the movement to create the world of tomorrow and to enrich the content of human life.

The unfinished revolution can reach fulfillment if we have faith and confidence in ourselves and the assurance that however long and arduous the journey ahead we shall reach our destination.

DECLARATION ON PEACE, INDEPENDENCE, DEVELOPMENT, COOPERATION AND DEMOCRATIZATION OF INTERNATIONAL RELATIONS

The third conference of heads of state or government of the following non-aligned countries was held in Lusaka, Zambia, from 8th to 10th September, 1970. The following countries were present:

Afghanistan, Algeria, Botswana, Burundi, Cameroun, Central African Republic, Ceylon, Chad, Congo (Brazzaville), Congo (Kinshasa), Cuba, Cyprus, Equatorial Guinea, Ethiopia, Gabon, Ghana, Guinea, Guyana, India, Indonesia, Iraq, Jamaica, Jordan, Kenya, Kuwait, Laos, Lebanon, Lesotho, Liberia, Libya, Malaysia, Mali, Mauritania, Morocco, Nepal, Nigeria, Rwanda, Senegal, Sierra Leone, Singapore, Somalia, Sudan, Swaziland, Syria, Tanzania, Togo, Trinidad and Tobago, Tunisia, Uganda, United Arab Republic, Yemen Arab Republic, Yugoslavia and Zambia.

The following countries attended as observers:

Argentina, Barbados, Bolivia, Brazil, Chile, Colombia, Peru, South Vietnam, Venezuela.

The Secretary General of the Organization of African Unity also attended as an observer.

The following national liberation movements addressed the Conference as guests:

ANC (African National Congress—South Africa), FRELIMO, FLCS (French Somalia), MPLA (Angola), MOLI-

NACO (Comora Islands), Palestine Liberation Movement and
ZAPU and ZANU (Zimbabwe).

1. They exchanged views on the significance and the role
of non-aligned countries in the present world, with particular
reference to safeguarding and strengthening world peace and
security, ensuring national independence and full sovereignty
of all nations on a basis of equality, on the need to realize
the fundamental right of all peoples to self-determination, as
well as democratization of international relations, promoting
the rapid economic growth of the developing countries and
considering possibilities for greater consultation and cooperation among the non-aligned countries and strengthening the
United Nations.

2. Two and a half decades ago, the peoples of the United
Nations inscribed in the Charter their desire to save succeeding generations from the scourge of war; to reaffirm faith
in fundamental human rights, in the dignity of the human
person, in the equal rights of nations, large and small; to
establish conditions under which justice and respect for obligations arising from treaties and other sources of international
law can be maintained and to promote social progress and
better standards of life in larger freedom for all. The inter-
vening period has confirmed the historic merit of these ideals
and aspirations but it has likewise demonstrated that many
expectations have not been fulfilled and many problems have
not been solved, notwithstanding the efforts of the non-aligned
countries.

3. The policy of non-alignment has emerged as the result
of the determination of independent countries to safeguard
their national independence and the legitimate rights of
their peoples. The growth of non-alignment into a broad
international movement cutting across racial, regional and
other barriers is an integral part of significant changes in
the structure of the entire international community. This is
the product of the world anti-colonial revolution and of the
emergence of a large number of newly liberated countries

which, opting for an independent political orientation and development, have refused to accept the replacement of centuries-old forms of subordination by new ones. At the root of these changes lies the ever more clearly expressed aspiration of nations for freedom, independence and equality, and their determination to resist all forms of oppression and exploitation. This has been the substance and meaning of our strivings and actions; this is a confirmation of the validity of the Belgrade and Cairo declarations. At a time when the polarization of the international community on a bloc basis was believed to be a permanent feature of international relations, and the threat of a nuclear conflict between the big powers an ever-present specter hovering over mankind, the non-aligned countries opened up new prospects for the contemporary world and paved the way for relaxation of international tension.

4. Our era is at the crossroads of history; with each passing day we are presented with fresh evidence of the exceptional power of the human mind and also of the dangerous paths down which its imperfections may lead. The epoch-making scientific and technological revolution has opened up unlimited vistas of progress; at the same time, prosperity has failed to become accessible to all and a major section of mankind still lives under conditions unworthy of man. Scientific discoveries and their application to technology have the possibility of welding the world into an integral whole, reducing the distance between countries and continents to a measure making international cooperation increasingly indispensable and ever more possible; yet the states and nations comprising the present international community are still separated by political, economic and racial barriers. These barriers divide countries into developed and the developing, oppressors and the oppressed, the aggressors and the victims of aggression; into those who act from positions of strength, either military or economic, and those who are forced to live in the shadow of permanent danger of covert and overt as-

saults on their independence and security. In spite of the great progressive achievements and aspirations of our generation, neither peace, nor prosperity, nor the right to independence and equality, have yet become the integral, indivisible attribute of all mankind. Our age, however, raises the greatest hopes and also presents the greatest challenges.

5. The immediate danger of a conflict between the super powers has lessened because their tendency to negotiate in their mutual relations is strengthening; however, it has not yet contributed to the security of the small, medium-sized and developing countries, or prevented the danger of local wars.

6. The practice of interfering in the internal affairs of other states, and the recourse to political and economic pressure, threats of force and subversion are acquiring alarming proportions and dangerous frequency. Wars of aggression are raging in the Middle East and in Indochina and being prolonged in South Vietnam and extended to Cambodia and the presence of foreign forces in Korea is posing a threat to national independence and international peace and security. The continued oppression and subjugation of the African peoples in southern Africa by the racist and colonial minority regimes, apart from being a blot on the conscience of mankind, poses a serious threat to international peace and security. This situation is becoming dangerously explosive as a result of the collusion between certain developed countries of the West and the racist minority regimes in this part of the world. The continuing arms race is causing alarm and concern and rendering nuclear detente extremely precarious and serves as a spur to limited wars. The balance of terror between the super powers has not brought peace and security to the rest of the world. There are welcome signs of a growing detente between the power blocs but the abatement of the cold war has not yet resulted in the disintegration of the military blocs formed in the context of great power conflicts.

7. International relations are entering a phase charac-

terized by increasing interdependence and also by the desire of states to pursue independent policies. The democratization of international relations is therefore an imperative necessity of our times. But there is an unfortunate tendency on the part of some of the big powers to monopolize decision-making on world issues which are of vital concern to all countries.

8. The forces of racism, apartheid, colonialism and imperialism continue to bedevil world peace. At the same time classical colonialism is trying to perpetuate itself in the garb of neo-colonialism—a less obvious, but in no way a less dangerous, means of economic and political domination over the developing countries. These phenomena of the present-day world tend not only to perpetuate the evils of the past but also to undermine the future; they retard the liberation of many countries still under colonial domination and jeopardize the independence and territorial integrity of many countries, above all of the non-aligned and developing countries, hampering their advancement, intensifying tension and giving rise to conflicts.

9. The economic gap between the developed and the developing countries is increasingly widening—the rich growing richer and the poor remaining poor. The developing countries are being denied their right to equality and to effective participation in international progress. The technological revolution, which is now the monopoly of the rich, should constitute one of the main opportunities for progress of developing countries. World solidarity is not only a just appeal but an overriding necessity; it is intolerable today for some to enjoy an untroubled and comfortable existence at the expense of the poverty and misfortune of others.

10. Concerned by this state of affairs in the world, the participants in this conference have agreed to take joint action, and to unite their efforts towards that end.

11. The participants in the conference of non-aligned countries reaffirm and attach special importance to the following principles: The right of the peoples who are not yet

free to freedom, self-determination and independence; respect for the sovereignty and territorial integrity of all states; the right of all states to equality and active participation in international affairs; the right of all sovereign nations to determine in full freedom the paths of their internal political, economic, social and cultural development; the right of all peoples to the benefits of economic development and the fruits of the scientific and technological revolution; refraining from the threat or use of force, and the principle of peaceful settlement of disputes.

12. The conference declares that the following continue to be the basic aims of non-alignment: the pursuit of world peace and peaceful co-existence by strengthening the role of non-aligned countries within the United Nations so that it will be a more effective obstacle against all forms of aggressive action and the threat or use of force against the freedom, independence, sovereignty and territorial integrity of any country; the fight against colonialism and racialism which are a negation of human equality and dignity; the settlement of disputes by peaceful means; the ending of the arms race followed by universal disarmament; opposition to great-power military bases and foreign troops on the soil of other nations in the context of great-power conflicts and colonial and racist suppression; the universality of and the starting of strengthening of the efficacy of the United Nations; and the struggle for economic independence and mutual cooperation on a basis of equality and mutual benefit. What is needed is not redefinition of non-alignment but a rededication by all non-aligned nations to its central aims and objectives.

13. The participants in the conference solemnly declare that they shall consistently adhere to these principles in their mutual relations and in their relations with other states. They have accordingly agreed to take the following measures:

a) To achieve full solidarity and to initiate effective and concrete measures against all forces that jeopardize and violate the independence and territorial integrity of the non-aligned countries and in this purpose to cooperate with and consult each other as and when necessary;

b) to continue their efforts to bring about the dissolution of great-power military alliances in the interest of promoting peace and relaxing international tensions, under circumstances ensuring the security of all states and peoples; to safeguard international peace and security through the development of social, economic, political and military strength of each country;

c) to assert the right of all countries to participate in international relations on an equal footing which is imperative for the democratization of international relations;

d) to offer determined support to the intensification of the work of all international bodies concerned with problems of disarmament, particularly in the preparations for and implementation of the program of the disarmament decade as an integral part of general and complete disarmament;

e) to intensify and unite efforts among the developing countries and between them and the developed countries for the carrying out of urgent structural changes in the world economy and for the establishment of such international cooperation as will reduce the gap between developed and developing countries;

f) to intensify joint efforts for the liquidation of colonialism and racial discrimination: to this end to pledge their utmost possible moral, political and material support to national liberation movements and to ensure implementation of international decisions, including measures by the Security Council in accordance with the relevant provisions of the United Nations Charter;

g) to continue their efforts towards strengthening the role and efficacy of the United Nations, to promote the achievement of the universality of the United Nations and the urgent need for giving the People's Republic of China her rightful place in the organization and the admission of other countries, still outside the United Nations, including those which are still divided, to participate in the activities of the organization and its agencies;

h) to strengthen steadily and expand the domain of mutual cooperation within the international, regional and bilateral frameworks;

i) to ensure the continuity of action by holding periodic consultations of representatives of non-aligned countries at different levels and by convening summit conferences more frequently depending on the prevailing international situation.

14. The heads of state or government and leaders of participating countries resolve that this declaration as well as the statements and resolutions issued by this conference shall be forwarded to the U.N. and brought to the attention of all the member states of the world organization. The present declaration shall also be forwarded to all other states.

15. The participants in the conference appeal to all nations and governments, all peace- and freedom-loving forces and to all people the world over for cooperation and joint efforts for the implementation of these objectives. At the same time, they declare that they shall support all international actions that are initiated in the interests of the progress of mankind.

DECLARATION ON NON-ALIGNMENT AND ECONOMIC PROGRESS

The heads of state or government of non-aligned countries, united by common political and economic aspirations,

Expressing the determination of the non-aligned countries to achieve economic emancipation, to strengthen their independence and to make their contribution to world peace and to economic and social progress for all mankind;

Reviewing the lack of progress in the implementation by the international community of the policies and objectives declared by them at Belgrade and Cairo, and those enshrined in the Charter of Algiers;

Disturbed by the rapidly widening gap between the economies of the rich and the poor nations, which constitutes a threat to the independence of developing countries and to international peace and security;

Noting with concern the negative trends which exclude developing countries in particular, the decline in the share of developing countries from the mainstream of world economic life despite their endeavor to participate in contemporary progress;

Noting in particular the decline in the share of developing countries in world export trade from one-third in 1950 to one-sixth in 1969;

Noting further with regret the decline in financial flows in terms of percentage of GNP from developed to developing countries and the increase in financial flows from developing countries by way of payments of debts, dividends, and royalties, and financial and commercial services;

Believing that the poverty of developing nations and their economic dependence on those in affluent circumstances constitute a structural weakness in the present world economic order;

Convinced that the persistence of an inequitable world economic system inherited from the colonial past and continued through present neo-colonialism poses insurmountable difficulties in breaking the bondage of poverty and shackles of economic dependence;

Realizing that the occupation of parts of territories of non-aligned developing countries and dependent nations by aggressors or minority governments deprives these groups of their resources and constitutes a hindrance to their development;

Considering that the gap in science and technology between the developing and developed countries is widening and the need for preventing the emergence of technological colonialism is pressing;

Recognizing that the massive investments in the economic and social progress of mankind can be made if agreements are reached to reduce expenditure on armaments;

Conscious of the increase since the meeting in Belgrade in the capability of non-aligned countries to plan, organize and manage their own economic development, both individually and within a multi-national cooperative framework, and the progress made by them during the sixties;

Convinced that the Second United Nations Development Decade provides an opportunity to bring about structural changes in the world economic system so as to meet the pressing needs of poor nations, to strengthen their independence, and to provide for a more rapid and better balanced expansion of the world economy;

A. Hereby pledge themselves

1) to cultivate the spirit of self-reliance and to this end to adopt a firm policy of organizing their own socio-economic

progress and to raise it to the level of a priority action program;

2) to exercise fully their right and fulfill their duty so as to secure optimal utilization of the natural resources on their territories and in adjacent seas for the development and welfare of their peoples;

3) to develop their technology and scientific capability to maximize production and improve productivity;

4) to promote social changes to provide increasing opportunity to each individual for developing his worth, maintaining his dignity, making his contribution to the process of growth and for sharing fully in its fruits;

5) to promote social justice and efficiency of production, to raise the level of employment and to expand and improve facilities for education, health, nutrition, housing and social welfare;

6) to ensure that external components of the developmental process further national objectives and conform to national needs; and in particular to adopt so far as practicable a common approach to problems and possibilities of investment of private capital in developing countries;

7) to broaden and diversify economic relationships with other nations so as to promote true interdependence;

B. Decide

to foster mutual cooperation among developing countries so as to impart strength to their national endeavor to fortify their independence;

to contribute to each other's economic and social progress by an effective utilization of the complementarities between their respective resources and requirements;

to intensify and broaden to the maximum extent practicable the movement for cooperation and integration among developing countries at sub-regional and inter-regional levels for accelerating their economic growth and social development and take into account the necessary measures required to guarantee that the peoples of developing countries concerned receive the benefit of the integration and not the foreign companies operating within the integrated area;

and to this end, to adopt the following program of action in the field of:

I. PLANNING AND PROJECTION

a) to identify products and countries in which production can be stimulated and expanded with a view to increasing existing income and trade exchange;

b) to identify projects and programs for which import requirements capable of being met from developing countries are likely to arise, and

c) to define as closely as possible financing and technological requirements to secure increases in production and to support expansion of trade flows among developing countries.

II. TRADE, COOPERATION AND DEVELOPMENT

a) to organize exchange of information in regard to products of export interest to developing countries;

b) to provide adequate access to products of export interest to other developing countries, especially by preferential reduction of import duties;

c) to negotiate long-term purchases and sale agreements in respect of industrial raw materials and to orient policies of official procurement organizations in favor of developing countries;

d) to evolve payment arrangements to support expansion of trade exchanges among developing countries;

e) to facilitate transit traffic for the diversification and the expansion of the external trade of landlocked countries;

f) to facilitate international traffic across overland transit highways crossing international borders among developing countries; and

g) to encourage travel and tourism among developing countries.

III. INDUSTRIAL, MINERAL, AGRICULTURAL AND MARINE PRODUCTION

a) to exchange information on needs and resources of different developing countries in respect of technical know-how, research, consultancy services, experts and training facilities; and

b) to institute and intensify programs of cooperation at bilateral, regional and inter-regional levels to combine needs and resources of developing countries for furthering one another's production programs and projects;

c) to coordinate through policies and measures for the utilization in their national interest their mineral and marine resources and for the protection of the maritime environment.

IV. DEVELOPMENT OF INFRASTRUCTURE

a) to facilitate mutual cooperation in preparing pre-investment and investment surveys and in executing projects for the development of one another's infrastructure in the field of road and rail communication, irrigation and power; and

b) to concert measures for transforming the prevailing systems of communications, transport and commercial services previously designed to link metropolitan countries to their dependent territories so as to promote direct commerce, contact and cooperation among developing countries.

V. APPLICATION OF SCIENCE AND TECHNOLOGY

a) to organize means and measures to share one another's experience in the application of science and technology to processes of economic and social development;

b) to institute schemes of cooperation for the acquisition of skills relevant to their situation and in particular to promote exchange of trainees and experts and thus provide for optimum use and efficiency of their specialized technological and scientific institutions; and

c) to devise programs for adoption of technology to the special needs of countries in different stages of development, and to provide for its widest possible diffusion to developing countries and for the conservation of their technical skills and personnel in consonance with their needs and conditions.

VI. MECHANISM

to facilitate contact, exchange of information, coordination and consultations among governments and concerned organizations and institutions to further mutual cooperation and integration for implementing the programs of action;

C. Urge the United Nations

to fulfill the objectives enshrined in the Charter "to promote social progress and better standards of life in larger freedom";

to employ international machinery to bring about a rapid transformation of the world economic system, particularly in the fields of trade, finance and technology so that economic domination yields to economic cooperation and economic strength is used for the benefit of the world community;

to view the developmental process in a global context and to adopt a program of international action for utilization of world resources in men and materials, science and technology, benefiting developed and developing countries alike;

to adopt at their commemorative meeting a declaration on the international strategy providing for the following:

I. GOALS AND OBJECTIVES

a) International cooperation for economic development is not a one-sided process of donor-donee relationship; the development of developing countries is a benefit to the whole world, including the more advanced nations;

b) The aim of international economic cooperation should be to provide a dynamic combination of the world's production, market and technological factors to promote a rational division of labor and a humane sharing of its fruits; international cooperation should strengthen the capability of developing countries to exercise fully their sovereignty over their natural resources;

c) A rapid transformation of the world economic system should be achieved through the adoption of convergent and concomitant policies and measures so that the developing and developed countries become partners, on a basis of equality and mutual benefit, in a common endeavor for peace, progress and prosperity;

d) The essential purpose of development is to provide equal opportunity for a better life to everyone; the aim should, therefore, be to accelerate significantly the growth of gross product per head so that it is possible to secure for everyone a minimum standard of life consistent with human dignity;

II. POLICIES AND MEASURES

a) Since primary commodities constitute a preponderant source of foreign income for most developing countries, provision should be made for maximizing their consumption, diversifying their utilization, securing for producers a fair and equitable return, organizing their production on the basis of endowment factors, and securing for developing countries an increasing share of the growth in consumption; unfinished action to conclude commodity agreements should be completed by 1972;

b) International action should be taken to promote processing of primary products in areas of production and to provide access to consuming markets of processed products, free from all tariff and non-tariff barriers;

c) The scheme of non-discriminatory non-reciprocal preferences in favor of products of developing countries is implemented without further delay;

d) Other measures should be undertaken to secure for developing countries an increasing share of international trade in manufactured and semi-manufactured goods, especially through adjustment of production structures in developed countries;

e) A distinction should be made between transfer of resources intended to promote development of developing countries and commercially motivated investments;

f) The new flow of financial transfers from developed to developing countries should correspond, by 1972, to a minimum of one per cent of the GNP of each developed country, three-fourths of which should be from official sources;

g) Financial transfer for development should be united and provided on terms and conditions compatible with the efficiency of the developmental progress;

h) Appropriate measures should be adopted to alleviate the burden of debts on developing countries;

i) A link between special drawing rights and development finance should be established by 1972;

j) Steps should be taken to enable developing countries to extend their merchant marines, to develop their shipbuilding industries and to improve and modernize their ports. Urgent action is needed to restrain the alarming increase in freight rates and to eliminate discriminatory and restrictive elements from it. Consultation machinery for the solution of difficulties of shippers from developing countries needs to be improved to increase its efficiency;

k) Concerted measures should be undertaken to bridge the widening gap in the technological skills between developing and developed countries, to facilitate diffusion of technology, patented and non-patented, on reasonable terms and conditions, and to ensure that transfers of technology are free from illegitimate restraints. An appropriate international mechanism should be devised to implement these measures;

l) Provision should be made to expand research and development on materials with which developing countries are endowed. Arrangements should also be made for their nationals and institutions to build up scientific capabilities;

m) Within the framework of international development strategy, special measures should be taken to improve the productive capacities and develop the infrastructure of least developed, including landlocked countries, so as to enable them to derive full benefit from convergent and concomitant measures; and

n) Mutual contact and cooperation among developing countries is an indispensable element in the global strategy. The developed countries should support the initiative of developing countries in this regard and pay special attention to concrete proposals that may be put forward by them to this end.

D. Declare their determination

a) to undertake sustained and continuous endeavors within the United Nations system to secure faithful implementation of international development policies and programs;

b) to further the unity and solidarity of the group of seventy-seven at all levels, including the convening of a ministerial meeting to prepare for UNCTAD 3;

c) to review and appraise periodically the progress of mutual cooperation in the field of development in pursuance of the program of action;

d) to seek ways and means for strengthening the capabilities of the United Nations system to fulfill its commitments to social and economic progress.

Index

A

Addis Ababa conferences, 70, 145, 146.
Aden, 76, 89, 99, 122.
Afghanistan, 53, 114, 181.
Africa, 5, 14, 22, 28, 33, 34, 49, 54, 55, 60, 69, 71, 78, 83, 84, 94, 99, 100, 109, 110, 119, 132, 134, 150, 151, 152, 153, 159, 160, 174, 184. *See also* African Unity, Organization of; Algeria; Congo (Kinshasa); Portugal and related listings; Tunisia; Union of South Africa and related listings.
African Unity, Organization of, 84, 89, 109, 114, 118, 120, 121, 123, 125, 126, 146, 154, 173, 181. *See also* Africa.
Alexandria conference, 69.
Algeria, 21, 23, 25, 48, 53, 59, 71, 87, 114, 181. *See also* France.
Algiers, Charter of, 189.
Angola, 21, 23, 25, 49, 59, 84, 89, 110, 114, 119, 120, 152, 153, 173, 181. *See also* Portugal.
apartheid, 49, 60, 89, 102, 110, 116, 123–125, 138, 152, 173, 177, 185. *See also* Union of South Africa.
Arab States, League of, 114.
Argentina, 114, 181.
Asia, 5, 14, 22, 28, 33, 34, 54, 55, 60, 78, 93, 98–99, 100, 113, 119, 132, 134, 150, 174. *See also* Southeast Asia.

B

Bandung conference, 5, 33, 70, 80, 123, 125.
Bantustans, 153. *See also* Union of South Africa.
Barbados, 181.
Belgrade conference, vii, 3–65, 70, 71, 72, 79, 80, 83, 84, 85, 86, 87, 91, 92, 98, 100, 101, 105, 108, 114, 115, 117, 123, 125, 134, 136, 137, 147, 161, 169, 183, 189, 190.
Berlin, 21, 30, 43–44, 45, 65, 101. *See also* divided nations; Germany.
Bizerta, 4, 23, 48, 71. *See also* France; Tunisia.
Bolivia, 53, 114, 181.
Botswana, 181.
Brazil, 53, 114, 181.
British Guiana, 89, 122. *See also* Guyana.
Burma, 53, 114.
Burundi, 114, 118, 181.

C

Cairo conference, vii, 69–141, 147, 154, 155, 161, 183, 189.
Cambodia, 53, 93, 99, 103, 114, 129, 163, 176, 184. *See also* Southeast Asia.
Cameroon, 114, 181.
Caribbean area, 113, 123, 174. *See also* Cuba.

D
839
.2
.C65

48029

Conference of Heads of State
or Government of Non-aligned
Countries.
Neither East or West.

DATE DUE